BECOMING WHOLE

BECOMING WHOLE

A "Whole Person – Whole World" Workbook exploring HOW to become Whole, through embracing and understanding our mind, body, feelings and spirit.

Wrekin Trust

in Association with the Wrekin Trust

Emma Mary Gathergood

Becoming Whole
Emma Mary Gathergood

Published by Greyhound Self-Publishing 2015
Malvern, Worcestershire, United Kingdom.

Printed and bound by Aspect Design
89 Newtown Road, Malvern, Worcs. WR14 1PD
United Kingdom
Tel: 01684 561567
E-mail: allan@aspect-design.net
Website: www.aspect-design.net

A copy of this book has been deposited with the British Library Board

ISBN 978-1-909219-23-6

This book is dedicated to my great inspiration Sir George Trevelyan and the work of the Wrekin Trust, past, present and future.

It is also dedicated to my lovely family which includes my three children, Alexander, Daniel and Lucy, their partners, my 7 beautiful grandchildren Jordan, Phoenix, Leah, Storm, Levi, Raphael and Isis, and their grandfather, Richard.

I would also like to thank Claire Haddock and Shabra Dowson for the great help they have given me in proof reading the manuscript.

Contents

Introduction

In May 2014 a spiritual teacher from the United States was in my locality running a workshop. We, at the Wrekin Trust, and others had agreed upon the title of the workshop "Whole Person – Whole World" six months earlier and I was looking forward to learning more about this special subject…. one so close to my heart.

Towards the end of the weekend the teacher was asked by a participant "So how ***do*** you become a Whole Person?" Due to time restraints and other questions being posed that question did not get answered, and something in me stirred.

I instinctively knew in that moment that it was not the teacher's job, but ***my*** job to answer this question. How ***do*** we become whole people, and so start to create a whole world? I had been present at the Wrekin Trust planning meeting in October 2013 when we were looking for a focus for our next year's work. And when the phrase "Whole Person – Whole World" was suggested I literally jumped out of my chair, exclaiming "That's it! That sums it up perfectly!" I knew in that instant this phrase also described my life's work.

I had retired from the NHS and my work as a therapist in the field of mental health a few years earlier after a career spanning more than forty years. I had already written and published a book called "Holistic Therapy – Overcoming Depression and Anxiety Naturally" as I was approaching my retirement.

Now I had expanded my work by joining forces with the Wrekin Trust to take my wholistic approach beyond mental health out into the arena of evolutionary consciousness, personal growth, spiritual development, environmental awareness, holistic life coaching, whole body consciousness and wholistic well-being.

So the day following the workshop I e-mailed all the participants, inviting them to come to a fortnightly Study Group where we answered the question "So ***how*** do we become a whole person, able to create a whole world?" I also emailed other friends and colleagues to join us. I had already asked my dear friend and colleague Tessa Maskell if we could run the group from her house, as it was larger and more centrally placed in Great Malvern than my little garden flat on the side of the Malvern Hills.

She had readily agreed and so on May 20th 2014 we ran the first of a 10 part Wrekin Trust Study Group. Most weeks we had between 10 and 12 people present and the group bonded so well that when it ended almost everyone opted to continue to meet fortnightly, but now as a leaderless Support and Development Group, where they continued to apply the learnings and experiences from the Study Group, whilst studying many other relevant and interesting subjects. It is still running, with several new and deeply supportive relationships having started between the participants.

This book is my attempt to turn the Study Group Course notes into a work-book that can be used by others wishing to develop along these lines. I sincerely hope it achieves its purpose and I manage to convey some of the love and support that grew up between everyone as the course progressed.

Thank you to all who made this experience possible and especially to Tessa for her continuous encouragement, support, enthusiasm and intelligent questioning that enabled me to grow as a teacher and facilitator way beyond what I was when I started teaching the course! Without her this whole experience could not have happened, the course notes would not have been written and this book would not be here now!

In order to make best use of this workbook, buy yourself a special exercise book or journal, where you can write up all the exercises as you do them, in order to keep them all in one place, and be able to refer back to what you have written. This will help you to be able to see how far you have progressed in your awareness after you have completed the book.

Emma Mary Gathergood
West Malvern, March 2015

Chapter One
The Wholistic Map Part I: Working Wholistically

This book is all about taking a journey into wholeness. No matter **who** you are or **where** you are on your journey, or even if you are not aware you are on a journey, you can benefit from this simple but whole way of looking at life. We all have a body, mind, feelings and spirit, and as such will benefit from understanding **how** to work with all that we are, in order to become more true to ourselves, experience more well-being, and become able to fulfil our potential, becoming a powerful force for good in the world.

Surely our aim at this crucial time in human history is to individually experience, become, and model, BEING a whole person, and in being that, contribute to the development of a whole world. As we move from ego based behaviours to an ability to come from our True Self to quote Gandhi, we can "become the change we want to see in the world".

So how do we do that?

We know that in order to be a whole person we need to equally embrace, nurture and heal the four aspects of our human being; body, feelings, mind and spirit. In doing so, we become more effective as individuals, empowering others and ourselves to reach our full potential, through our personal relationships and extended community.

We are equally aware of the need to move to a more sustainable ecological lifestyle. This includes raising consciousness about environmental issues, the rights of nature, climate change and its consequences, collective greed and world poverty in order to grow a whole world for future generations to enjoy.

What could be more relevant in the present climate of unrest than the prophetic words of Wrekin Trust's founder Sir George Trevelyan back in the 1970s, ***"This is the emergence of a new humanity.... We recognise an evolutionary thrust towards a higher consciousness for humanity, unlocking spiritual potential hitherto dormant".***[1] But how is this new humanity going to emerge? Is it through laws being passed or great books being written? Is it through wonderful conferences, where we fly half way around the world to hear the latest authority telling us about the changes happening?

No, the new humanity will start to emerge when you and I start to think, feel, behave and BE different!

If we want to see a whole world, a world where all forms of life are respected, what are you and I going to do about it? How can **WE** become whole people? How can **WE** become part of the "evolutionary thrust towards a higher consciousness for humanity"? What about you and me? What can **WE** do?

Let's start with looking at our mind and how we think! Yes we may well meditate every day, and for that short period of time we are able to still our mind and experience oneness and peace, but what do we think about during our remaining waking hours? Are our minds taken over with worry, with negative thinking, with blaming, criticising, judging and complaining? Would it help if we learnt how to become mindful of our thoughts? What if we stopped ourselves before our minds ran away with themselves, took a step back and just watched our thoughts as we might watch the clouds scurrying across the sky? Just by doing this simple exercise throughout the day, we are able to put some distance between us and our thoughts, helping us to see the fact that **we HAVE thoughts, but we are MORE than our thoughts!**

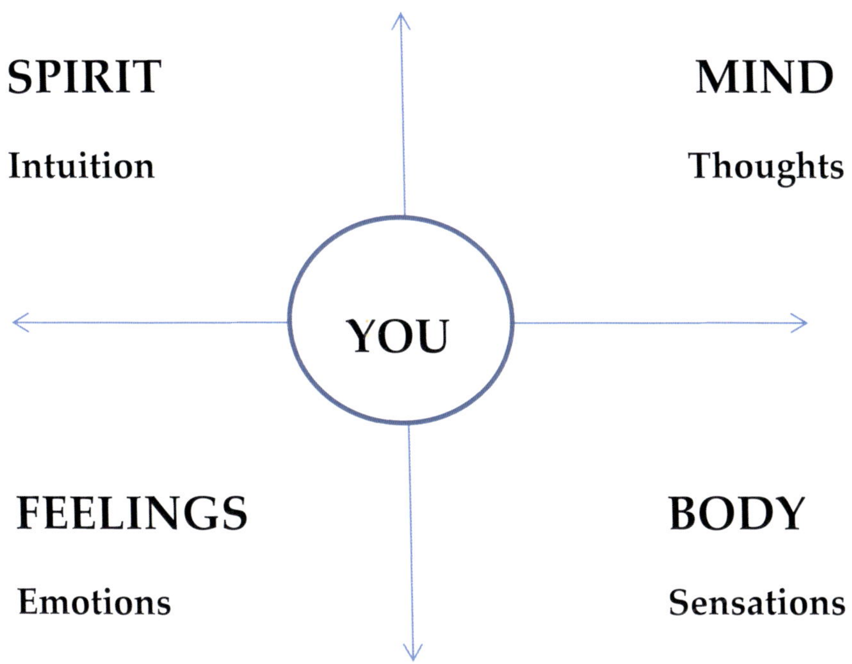

Fig.1

Can we pause for a moment and look at Fig 1 the Wholistic Map above. Imagine if you were asked to put a small cross in each of the four squares in order to indicate where your consciousness is at this point in your personal journey, whereabouts would you place them?

Starting with the “Mind” section, would you place your cross near or even in the central circle, indicating that your mind is influenced by your **TRUE SELF**, and is not running away with itself, and is always able to be self-reflective and aware? Or do you feel quite often your mind seems to have a “mind of its own”, despite your daily attempts at stilling the mind through meditative practice, so you may place your little cross near the letter “d” of the word “Mind”? Or do you feel you have no control over your mind whatsoever, and feel your cross needs to be placed way out in the margin of the page?

Spend a few moments contemplating this question, totally without any self-judgement or blame prior to making your mark, either on this page of the book, or draw out the map in your journal and add your cross in the Mind section. Then become aware that your mind is only a part of who you are, not the totality of yourself.

Then we can look at our body and our behaviour. Is our body relaxed and at ease most of the day? Or do we perpetually have a knotted stomach, a tight chest, closed fists, hunched shoulders or a frown? If our body is all knotted up with tension, we are more likely to lash out either physically or with words without even realising what we are doing. Or if we are aware of not being aggressive to others, we may unconsciously be lashing out at ourselves, through personal "put-downs" or self-criticism.

Are we enjoying our bodies? Are we celebrating our physicality by feeding ourselves healthy, nutritious food, and taking pleasurable exercise? Are we spending time in nature, celebrating the seasons, and marvelling at the beautiful planet we have been given as our playground? **Yes we HAVE a body, but surely we are MORE than our body!**

Returning to the Wholistic Map and moving on to the "Body" section, would you place your cross near or even in the central circle, indicating that you are able to really honour and care for your Body, having your Body closely aligned to your **TRUE SELF?** This would imply you are always respectful of your Body's needs, understanding of its possible aging issues, and grateful of its magnificent automatic and largely unconscious abilities, like breathing and digestion.

Or do you feel quite often you are a little hard on your body, blaming it for not looking exactly the way you want it to, or criticising it for not being as fit as it used to be, so you may place your little cross near the letter "n" at the end of the word "Sensation"? Or do you feel distant from your body, treating it like a machine, paying it little attention or offering it little love and appreciation, and feel your cross needs to be placed way out in the margin of the page?

Then we can look at our feelings. What is our default setting, in regard to our feelings? Yes of course when something has really bothered us, we are going to have a reaction, which is natural and healthy. But when nothing is particularly affecting us for good or ill, what are our habitual feelings? Do we relax into a sense of peace and oneness, or are we looking for something that is wrong in our world, in order for us to return to our habitual anxiety, anger, resentment, hurt, depression or guilt? Taking a step back and becoming mindful of our feelings can put us in a place of choice. Do we really want to spend the rest of our lives feeling the way we feel right now? **Yes we HAVE feelings, but surely we are MORE than our feelings!**

Returning to the Wholistic Map again and moving on to the "Feelings" section, would you place your cross near or even in the central circle, indicating that your feelings are closely in touch with your **TRUE SELF**, and you are always able to accept, honour and work with your feelings in an open, trusting and loving way? Or do you feel quite often you are unaware of your true feelings, or find it easier to suppress or ignore them, so you may place your little cross near the letter "E" at the beginning of the word "Emotion"? Or do you feel that your feelings and emotions are often totally out of control, and feel your cross needs to be placed way out in the margin of the page?

Now we come to the fourth of our holistic functions, our spirit. Who are we BEING? Are we being our True Self, the part the Quakers call "the little bit of God in everyone", the part of ourselves that we meet in deep contemplation and prayer? Or is that part confined to the meditation stool or church, but inappropriate in the boardroom or family living room?

Finally returning to the Wholistic Map for the last time and moving on to the "Spirit" section, would you place your cross near or even in the central circle, indicating that you really know yourself to be your **TRUE SELF**, and you are always able to hear and respond to "the still small voice" of Spirit? Or do you feel quite often you forget about your **TRUE SELF's** perspective, coming from a less than ideal part of yourself in your decisions or behaviour, so you may place your little cross near the letter "S" at the beginning of the word "Spirit"? Or do you feel that you are far too busy and really haven't got time for all that spiritual nonsense, and so feel your cross needs to be placed way out in the margin of the page?

There is a concept that I want to introduce here and that is **"Primal Spirituality"**. A colleague and friend of mine, David Karchere, the Spiritual Director at Sunrise Ranch, Colorado was the first person I ever heard use this phrase and it speaks very deeply to me. It implies that when we are born we arrive in this world already connected to the Source, to Love, to God/Goddess/All-That-Is, Great Spirit (the name is irrelevant). We come in with an awareness of who we are and where we are in the great scheme of things. We are deeply connected to our own Primal Spirituality, and within that we have everything we need inside of us for our sojourn here.

However, as we grow and start to listen to those around us, our parents, teachers, peers, siblings, priests, vicars, media,

TV, films etc we are told something completely different. We are constantly bombarded with the fact that we are not good enough. We need to be smarter, prettier, richer, fatter, thinner, taller, shorter, darker, lighter, quieter, noisier, cleverer, more humble, more assertive, less selfish, happier, the list varies as to which culture we are born into. But in most cultures, apart from some indigenous tribes, we are all given the message we need to be different than we are, as we are not good enough the way we are.

Einstein said ***"Problems cannot be solved by the same level of thinking that created them."***[2] So if we want to start to solve our problems, both personal and global, it is essential we start to change ourselves. Looking at ourselves in this wholistic way, we can start to see how becoming mindful of our thoughts, words and deeds can indeed help us to become a whole person, and can in Sir George's words enable ***"the emergence of a new humanity…."***

When we look at the recent work of Ken Wilber, Craig Hamilton, Andrew Cohen and other evolutionary teachers, they tell us that we are the first generation who is able to evolve consciously. Up until this point in human evolution, the whole concept of evolution has been an unconscious affair, connected with the survival of the fittest. Now however the ones who will survive are not necessarily the fittest, but the ones who are able to behave in ways that allow the whole to flourish. In earlier times it was our physical prowess that enabled our genes to survive to subsequent generations.

The only way humans can now survive is if we evolve our consciousness, becoming what Barbara Marx Hubbard calls "**Humanis Universalis**", the universal human[3]. This human is far more interested in the survival of the whole, than in just their own personal survival, realising that we really are all one. What improves life for one, truly improves life for all, as ultimately there is no separation. Short term, ego-centric goals have to be replaced by goals that enable all to flourish. These changes in how we as individuals think, feel, behave and be, are the essential changes that humanity needs to make if we are to survive and prosper. The universal human behaves in ways that allow harmonious family living, a loving, caring community, and the development of a thriving, joyous whole world.

"Let there be peace on earth and let it begin with me!"

Exercise One

Creating your Wholistic Map

You may have already completed the exercise of creating your own personal Wholistic Map, showing exactly where you are on your journey to becoming a whole person at this moment in time. However if you haven't may I strongly suggest you stop reading and please create it now, preferably in a journal, with today's date against each of the four little crosses. It is important to realise the difference between reading about an exercise and actually doing it. We do not change, evolve and grow by reading about anything.

The actual experience of the doing of something filters down into our cells and is what changes us. We need to remember there is no shame, guilt or embarrassment needed if we see we are less evolved than we hoped we were! As an ancient Eastern proverb says "The journey of 1000 miles starts with the first step, and the only place to start on any journey, is from where we are right now". So create your own map lovingly accepting wherever you are right now, and knowing that as you work through this workbook, your position will change.

It will be important for you to return to this map throughout this course in order to mark your progress.

Meditation One :

Discovering "Who am I?"

Take a few deep breaths, and begin to relax your **BODY**. Starting with your toes, begin to concentrate on each part of your body in turn. Firstly as you breathe in become aware of your toes, then as you breathe out let go of tension in your toes, and allowing that part of the body to relax. Working up through your feet, ankles, calves, knees, thighs, buttocks, back, lower body, stomach area, chest, hands, arms, shoulders, neck, head and scalp, and so totally relaxing your entire body. Then say to yourself "**My body is PART of me, so I Have a Body but I am MORE than my body".**

Then think about your thoughts and your **MIND**. Start to become aware of your thoughts, watch them come into your field of awareness then watch them leave. Try to become an objective observer of your thoughts in this moment. So instead of getting caught up in your thoughts and running with them, for a while watch your thoughts come and go, just as if they were objects arising on a video screen. Watch them come and go with a detached awareness, totally without judgement or preference. Then say to your-self, "**My mind is part of me, so I HAVE a MIND but I am MORE than my mind**".

Then think about your **FEELINGS**. Become aware of any emotion you are experiencing, and just like in the earlier part of the exercise, attempt to become an impartial observer of your feelings. Don't get caught up in the highs or lows of your emotions, just witness what it is you are feeling. So name whatever feeling it is you are experiencing then just breathe it out, just as you did with the tension in your body. Then say to yourself, "**My feelings are part of me so I HAVE feelings but I am MORE than my feelings".**

Then finally allow yourself to sink down inside yourself, with a deep sense of peace and relaxation. It will have become apparent to you throughout this exercise that there is obviously a "**Detached Observer Self**" that has been doing the watching and making the statements about being more than your body, mind or feelings. This self is totally impartial, but is also kind, loving, warm, compassionate and caring. It definitely has your best interests at heart, and as you concentrate on its qualities, it does seem to be somehow bigger, more aware, more steady than any part of yourself you may have met before.

You can if you prefer, not attempt to name this part of you. But, if it feels good you can say, "**Yes, I am MORE than my body, mind and feelings. I am also an AWARE OBSERVER SELF, a Spiritual Being having an earthly experience, a wise self which is a part of and connected to the Whole".**

And before returning from your meditation, ask this Aware Self to show you a symbol, either a flower, plant, rock or something that is meaningful to you, to help you to remember this lovely relaxed comfortable feeling and to symbolise this essence of who you are. Then slowly stretch, open your eyes and return to here and now. Then write about your experience in your journal.

Chapter Two

The Wholistic Map Part II:
The Mask, The Shadow & The True Self

In this chapter we are looking at the second part of the model, and we will be working with both parts throughout this course. Indeed in the last chapter we will be putting these two parts together, to see how using the Wholistic Map can help us literally to "Become Whole"!

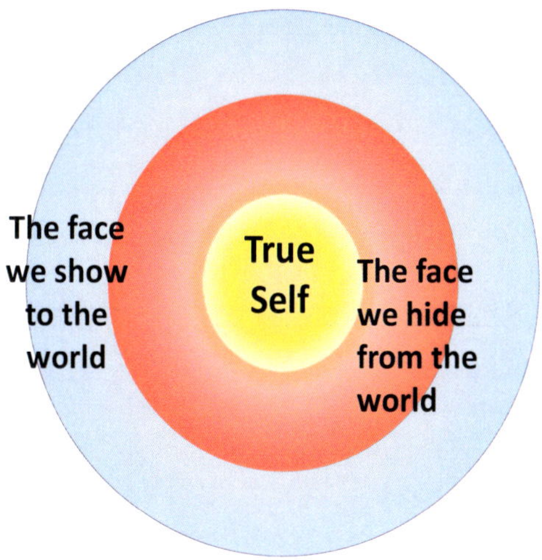

Fig 2

Looking at Figure 2, we can imagine our personality is made up of 3 layers, a little like Russian Dolls, each layer inside the other. The outer one represents "The Face we Show to the

World", the middle layer is "The Face we hide from the world", and the inside one is "The Face of WHO WE TRULY ARE", or our TRUE SELF.

Most of us, at some time in our life realise we need help because the outer layer, or the **Face we Show to the World** (known in psychological language as the **Mask Self**) is beginning to crumble. We are no longer able to choose to present a healthy face to the world. Something has happened in our life, which has meant there has been a feeling of the rug being pulled out from beneath us. We may have lost our way. Our once confident view of the world and our place in it has been shattered. We may be feeling insecure, anxious, lost, hopeless or depressed. What we want more than anything else is for someone to put us back together again, the way we used to be.

However, the more work we do on our own transformation, the more we begin to realise we are a bit like Humpty Dumpty, and cannot be put back together again, not now, not ever! Because the crisis has come to move us on to a new stage of development, and requires us to get to know parts of ourselves we either strongly dislike or deny, the "**Face we Hide from the World**", or in psychological language the **Shadow Self**. Not only that, the ME I think of as the real me, is not actually real at all, but an imitation or poor replica of my **TRUE SELF**.

As we work to understand and if necessary heal some of the unhelpful traits we find in our Shadow Self, and are also willing to see that we are definitely **more** than the qualities we find in either of these two layers, then we can begin to embrace the inner layer, which is actually the face of **Who We Really Are.** We may not be very familiar with this part of ourselves or it may be a face we don't know very well. Perhaps if we are a meditator we are able to reach this space during a good meditation, but few of us are able to consistently be this Self at will, or even really recognise what traits are in this inner layer.

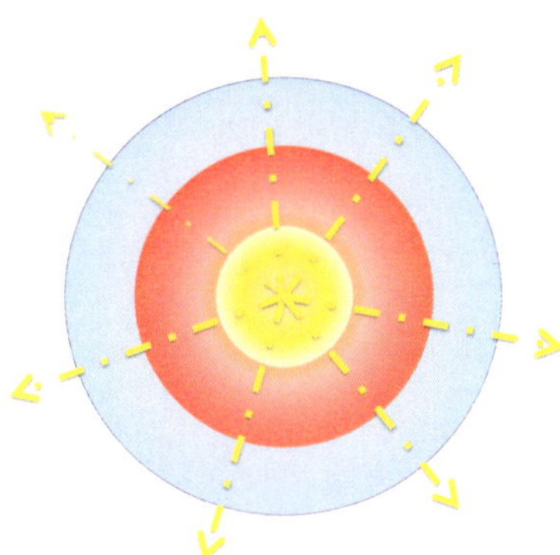

Fig.3

As we begin to embrace all parts of ourselves and daily connect to our own True Self, the wonderful truth of who we are starts to shine through (see Figure 3) It is as if we have turned on an inner light bulb inside ourselves, and this divine light starts to shine not only through the darker layers of our Shadow Self, transforming and healing them, but also out through our Mask Self and out into the world. People start to notice we are looking and acting differently.

There is a warmth, joy and authenticity about us that people actually feel when they are with us. We begin to raise the vibrations wherever we go, through "positive contagion", a phrase used both in finance and sport, to indicate how positivity spreads and becomes contagious in exactly the same way as negativity, fear and suspicion can rapidly spread through a crowd. We should not be surprised by this, as in truth we are all, indeed one! All people are actually connected when they are in their centre.

The reason I choose to use the term "True Self" rather than "Higher Self" is because to me, Higher Self gives a false impression of distance, loftiness and almost an unattainable sense of perfection. I myself worked with the concept of Higher Self for many years having first discovered it in my Psychosynthesis training, more than 35 years ago. However having worked both with my own process and with countless clients over the years, I now recognise that our **TRUE SELF** actually lives right inside our own being. It is not higher, or above us in any way. It is our core, our very Essence. So in calling it our **TRUE SELF**, we realise it is not separate from us in any way. So this terminology makes it more real, accessible, attainable and authentic.

Getting to know each layer

So we start by finding out what qualities are in each layer. What words would we use to describe our **MASK SELF** (represented by the Blue layer in Figures 2 & 3)? How do we like to present ourselves to the world? Do we like to be seen as intelligent, smart and professional? Or would we rather be seen as good fun, and great company? Maybe our identity is tied up with being nice, a people pleaser, a good person, reliable and kind? There are no rights and wrongs, when we list these qualities. **After all, this is not ACTUALLY who we are, but rather HOW WE LIKE TO BE SEEN!** But we often have so much riding on this definition of our self, we really believe these characteristics to be the truth of who we are.

However when we think about this model as if it were a set of Russian Dolls, we realise the only way to really understand what is going on in our inner world, is to spend time getting to know each layer in turn, starting with the outer one. Then, having learnt about those traits, we move on to getting to know the middle layer, the **SHADOW SELF** (portrayed as the red circle in Figures 2 & 3). So what words would we use to describe our Shadow Self? Are we frequently timid and fearful? Or do we have a tendency to be aggressive, critical or judgemental? Maybe we often end up becoming stuck in victimhood, feeling sorry for ourselves, and easily becoming depressed. Or are we devious and manipulative, or sometimes arrogant and superior?

We do this self-exploration with a sense of love and acceptance, realising whatever negative traits we find in this layer of ourselves have arrived there for good reason. We need to realise that often these so called negative traits **were actually essential in order for us to survive at an earlier stage of our development**. By this, we may mean during our own childhood, or youth, or we may mean this in a non-personal or larger context. When we realise that human nature has been developing and evolving over eons, we still have basic survival behaviour patterns in our DNA from the time when we ran from wild sabre-toothed tigers.

Many traits can be traced back to having developed at a time in our past (individually or collectively) when **that trait was essential for our survival**. These include our aggressive tendencies, our fear of the unknown, our desperate need to cling to the known, the status quo the safe, our sense of uselessness, our existential despair, our jealousy, guilt, arrogance, superiority, or indeed inferiority. We are not *bad* for having these traits, but we are probably living in a time warp, and **unconsciously reacting in ways that may once have served us**, but at this stage of our development are actually hindering our growth, and blocking us from becoming WHO WE REALLY ARE.

Once we have developed this healthy acceptance of our Shadow Self, we can start to look at the centre of our diagram. Our True Self is different from either our Mask Self or our Shadow Self and cannot be approached by thinking. **Our TRUE SELF is MORE than how we think**. We get to know this part of ourselves experientially. When we remember a time in our life when we were really being authentic, totally absorbed in and committed to what we were doing, we will be getting close.

We may have been out with friends, at work, alone in nature, caring for a pet or child, being creative or artistic, dancing, or lost in a reverie. Try to remember a time when you felt like this. Maybe a sense of peace, of belonging, of total involvement, of beauty, of love or oneness would describe this place. Qualities such as truth, commitment, healing, connection, belonging, passion, knowing, understanding, fully functioning, being the best we can be, authentic, excited, calm or serene could describe this place. We are all unique, and your **TRUE SELF** is authentic to you alone. Only you can really be *this* self, so no-one can tell you what qualities reside inside you.

So as we get to know our Mask, our Shadow and our True Self and as we start to take a microscope to our thinking, our feelings and our behaviour patterns with love, we begin to develop an open stance of true enquiry. If we can do this totally without judgment or criticism of what our investigations show us, we are bound to start to evolve, transform and change simply as a direct result of our sincere enquiry.

We definitely change more easily by following the carrot rather than the stick method! **It is totally counter-productive to berate ourselves (or indeed anyone else) for our failings and shortcomings**. As we start to work with this system we find something quite magical is starting to happen. We become aware that our **TRUE SELF** has some added value! It isn't just another layer of our personality; it is more like a light bulb. As we begin to spend time getting to know this Self it starts to shine. The light begins to radiate out, (Figure 3) straight through the heavy negative layer of our Shadow Self, totally unaffected by these negative vibes we experience in this layer, and out through our once cracked and disintegrating **MASK SELF**.

As a sage once said “Blessed are the Cracked, for they let in the Light!” And do we know why this happens? The reason for this metamorphosis is that when we reach our **TRUE SELF**, and begin to identify with the qualities we find there, we begin to feel a connection. This is firstly a connection with the earth. We begin to feel more grounded, more “in our bodies”, more earthed, solid, physically stronger, with less need to detach ourselves from others for our own protection, less isolated or alone, and as such more connected to and at one with our friends and family.

Secondly this is a connection with the “Ground of Being”, the Source, the Universe, Great Spirit, God/Goddess/All-That-Is, it matters not what we call it. All we know is, we are feeling connected with a Force greater than our own. We can even experiment with the feeling of being held in the arms of a loving, benevolent Universe, which actually loves us, supports us and wants to help and assist us.

Developing the courage to be fully ourselves is not about eliminating our negative traits, and reclaiming the Mask qualities we once held dear. On the contrary, it is **about getting to know, accept and love every part of ourselves**. It is about spending time in our Heart of Hearts, our **TRUE SELF**. If our inner self craves more alone time, being creative or being in nature, being with loved ones or animals, make that your top priority. Let this Self speak to you of its true hopes and dreams, desires, the way it wants to live, and decide to prioritise these needs, above the more superficial and changing ego needs of your personality.

The more time you spend in your inner self, the more you will be drawn to activities that enhance this part of yourself. Spending time meditating, doing yoga, tai chi, in quiet reverie, walking in nature, listening to beautiful uplifting music, will all help you to strengthen WHO YOU TRULY ARE. And the more this part is strengthened the more your light will start to shine out.

And by way of a bonus, your own intuition will start to develop. You will find yourself being aware of things beneath the surface in the lives of other people as well as in your own. Your own sense of inner wisdom will start to emerge. You will start to make more sensible choices, and react in less unconscious and automatic ways. In fact you will start to not only feel more whole, but also realise you are **becoming whole!**

Exercise Two:
The Three Faces of Self

*A. **The MASK: The outer face we show to the world***

1. How does this self like to behave & be seen?

2. What is the feeling associated with this behaviour?

3. What is your definition of life as seen from this place?
Life is ....

I am ....

Others are …..

4. How do you respond to life from within this mind-set?
First l ......

Then l .....

Then l .....

Later I ....

5. What does this self believe?

6. Where in the body is this self?

7. When you are thinking, feeling and behaving like this, about how old do you feel?

B. The SHADOW: The face we hide from the world

1. What are this self's behaviour patterns?

2. What is the feeling associated with this behaviour?

3. What is your definition of life as seen from this place?
Life is ....

I am ....

Others are …..

4. How do you respond to life from within this mind-set?
First l ......

Then l .....

Then l .....

Later I ....

5. What does this self believe?

6. Where in the body is this self?

7. When you are thinking, feeling and behaving like this, about how old do you feel?

C. THE FACE OF WHO YOU TRULY ARE

1. When you are coming from your Essence, how do you behave?

2. What is the feeling associated with this behaviour?

3. What is your definition of life as seen from this place?
Life is ....

I am ....

Others are .....

4. How do you respond to life from within this mind-set?
First I ......

Then I .....

Then I .....

Later I ....

5. What does this self believe?

6. Where in the body is this self?

7. Are you willing to allow this part of you to become the main voice you listen to in your life? Are you ready for the other selves to take a back seat and let your TRUE SELF shine through the rest of your personality, illuminating it from the inside?

Meditation Two:

The Russian Dolls

Close your eyes, then take three deep breaths, allowing yourself to breathe out slowly, letting your body relax deeply with each out-breath.

Imagine holding a set of 3 Russian Dolls in your hands. They are closed up with only the outer one visible. Your particular set of dolls is totally unique to you, not looking like any dolls you have ever seen before.

This outer doll represents the face you show to the world. It is your **Mask Self**, the way you like others to see you. How is it painted?.......... What are its traits?........

Send acceptance, love and support to this self.........

Then slowly imagine yourself opening it up and placing it down by your side. As you do so, be aware of some slightly negative energy emerging from the second doll. Do not be alarmed, this is all perfectly healthy and natural. This is the face you hide from the world, or your **Shadow Self**. Become aware of how it is painted and what are its traits. What don't you like people to know about you?......

Send acceptance, love and support to this self.........

Then slowly imagine yourself opening it up and placing it down by your side. Simultaneously be aware of light starting to pour out from the inner doll. Realise this glowing ball of light feels warm and pulsating in your hand.........

Know it is lit up from the inside, from a Source you cannot see, but can feel.......

Know this is your **True Self** ....

Feel the powerful, loving energy pulsating in your hands......

Know this is **Divine Energy**, this is your **Cosmic Spark** ....

Know this is **who you REALLY are.**

Take this Cosmic Spark with both hands and allow it to take form as a new Russian Doll, but this one is of your own design. This doll has the face of unconditional love, of total acceptance, of lifelong nurturing and support, of caring, understanding and devotion.

Allow her to become as strong and real as the dolls representing your Mask and Shadow Selves. Realise she is not only your inner light bulb, but she is also your Divine Spark, and she lives right next to your Shadow Self. She doesn't just accept all your foibles and issues, she totally understands, loves and welcomes them. She absolutely loves living next to your Shadow Self! She wants to live here! This is her job....this is her home! She totally accepts and loves all the traits she finds there.

How does it feel to know you are so totally loved and accepted?

What traits are here?........

What qualities do you feel within this glowing ball of light?..

Allow yourself to become this loving, connected being

Know this is **who you REALLY are**………

Take this Cosmic Spark with both hands and place it in your Heart Chakra

Know this is you!...........

And holding this Light in your heart, open your eyes and come back into the room. Then write about your experience in your journal.

Chapter Three

MIND I: Developing our Big Self

In this chapter we are concentrating on getting to know and understand our MIND, but probably in a way we have never looked at our mind before. In the first two chapters we looked at the two parts of the Wholistic Map and saw how body, mind, feelings and spirit are all related. So we are going to start now by allowing our spirit to influence our mind for the good by developing and growing a new helpful, positive and loving mind-set, which we will be calling "Big Self".

This is in contrast to our "Little Self" which is our often damaged and hurting emotional self. We will be working with this in a later chapter.

We will start by asking you to look at your current relationship with your mind. Do you like your mind? Do you trust it? Is it your best friend, a trusted ally? Or is it out of control, confusing, frustrating or irrational? It may be good to write a few notes in your journal to help you to recognise exactly how you do regard your mind at the moment.

Now, let's for a moment imagine how different your Mind would be if it was working in close union with your Spirit. What if your Mind wasn't constantly full of random thoughts picked up from your frightened or angry Little Self, or worse still picked up from the vast sea of negativity from the collective unconscious that is constantly swirling around our galaxy? What if the experience you had in the meditation in the first chapter became a reality and you could constantly be in the place of the Observer Self, watching and monitoring your thoughts, letting go of anything that is not positive and helpful?

Having established what your current relationship is with your mind, what would you like it to be? Write down your ideas, hopes and dreams for your Mind's development and evolution?

So how are you going to make this leap, from the current relationship you have with your mind to how you would like this relationship to be? Let us look for a moment at the physiology of the brain itself and how it develops.

Brain Development - Coercion, Competition or Co-operation

If our only way of protecting our vulnerable self as a child was to become a bully, in order to attempt to protect ourselves from the bullying we were in receipt of, then our Ego is probably coming from the most underdeveloped part of our brain, the Brain Stem, and our natural mode of being is **Coercion**.

We get our own way by being stronger than those around us, if not physically then by using the force of our will to get what we want. It feels natural for us to wield power over others, and we don't question our apparent leadership qualities in a macho type world. We are probably highly successful in the work place, becoming brilliant sales people or lawyers, and we enjoy wielding power.

Or alternatively, once we discovered we had a very good brain, or were excellent at sports, our way of getting our needs met was to **Compete**. We discovered we could usually win, because of our superior skill or brain power. Most of our educational methods here in the Western World are based in the Left Hemisphere of the brain, the part that controls logical and linear thinking, so it may feel quite natural to us to be competitive.

We are encouraged and rewarded by both parents and teachers to enjoy competing in the classroom and on the sports pitch. It is no surprise that the people our culture admires are the ones who are the best, the ones who win in the sports arena or on the TV or in films. So as we grow up we often continue this pattern in the workplace and often at home too, usually with dire consequences because competing with our partner is hardly the recipe for a long and happy marriage.

Or, it may be that neither coercing nor yet competing came naturally to us. We didn't get our kicks from either being the boss nor yet from winning. Maybe we feel more at home in the Right Hemisphere of the brain, the part that controls intuition and creativity, inspiration and reflection. The chosen mode we operate in and the one we are most comfortable in is coming from a sense of **Co-operation**.

So which of these three describes your natural way of being? It may be you started out with one, but have since evolved to another. If the chosen mode we operate in and the one we are most comfortable in is the one where we are coming from a sense of Co-operation, then we are actually the lucky ones. I know it doesn't actually feel like that. As some-one who has mainly come from this place, l know how difficult it is, and how we have often looked with longing at our apparently more successful fellows who are comfortable either coercing or competing. And if our aim is to succeed in the world as it functions at the moment, then yes, they are the lucky ones. But, as we are already seeing, that world is rapidly in decline. It is no longer functioning, and will continue to fall apart, making way for a new era and a new consciousness.

So those of us who have always wanted to co-operate have a head start and are more able to start to function with the new vibrations and energies that are forming in and around our planet at this deep time of transformation.

So this is where Big Self comes in to the equation! Our task is to help our Mind to mature through the developmental stages of coercion and competition to co-operation. And this does not only mean learning how to co-operate with others, this growth process actually starts **internally**.

We need to allow our Mind to start to understand, listen to, have empathy for, honour, respect and co-operate with our Little Self, with all its hang-ups and insecurities. And from this place of love and acceptance, we can start to work with Little Self, practising the art of T.L.C. or Tender Loving Care. The evolved Mind can grow into a Big Self who really cares for and looks out for us, just like a wise and loving parent, who always has our best interests at heart.

So how do we transform our Mind?

We transform it by getting to know it, by watching it in action and by being able to accurately name our behaviour patterns.

Don't be concerned if the traits you start to become aware of are less than ideal. Join the club! It is called the Human Condition. It is not personal to you. It is where humanity has got to at this stage of our evolution. We are not in this game to criticise ourselves but rather to love our selves better

OUR TRUE SELF LOVES US UNCONDITIONALLY!

And as we begin to learn about unconditional love from our True Self, we can begin to have this love for both our Mind and our Little Self. We can begin to feel ourselves floating in a warm sea of love and caring. We can develop a sense of being connected to a good and loving universe that has our best interests at heart.

We can also become aware that even if parts of our mind or feeling nature has some less than desirable traits, we can begin to react less, giving ourselves the chance to choose how we behave. For example if our natural reaction is to be bossy, we can step back and wait for someone else to take the lead on this occasion. Or if we tend to want to prove we are better at a given task then someone else, we can decide this time to kerb our competitive spirit and allow someone else to shine for a change. Or if we are more inclined to always take a back seat, maybe we can decide it is our moment to express our ideas and take the risk of speaking our truth. Our behaviour can change from automatic to aware and conscious.

But whatever changes we are seeking to make, we need to do it with a sense of respect for who we are. I once heard Oprah Winfrey say, "We do what we know how to do. When we know better we do better". We are not at fault or to blame for having negative traits. They simply developed because it was the best we could be at the time. Now we are learning about the power of choice, we can begin to change our less helpful behaviour patterns, by simply choosing another way of being. It won't be easy because these patterns are already well established. But it is no harder than learning a language or a skill such as piano playing or tennis.

And just as in attempting to learn a new skill we will learn more quickly and easily if we become a gentle and loving teacher to ourselves. In this case more carrot and less stick!

So how do we transform our Mind?

By loving it better!

Exercise Three
Developing our Big Self

You may have already done this, but if not, can you stop and answer these questions in your journal.

1. *What is your current relationship with your mind?*
2. *Do you like your mind? Do you trust it?*
3. *Is it your best friend, a trusted ally?*
4. *Or is it out of control, confusing, frustrating or irrational?*

Having established what your current relationship is with your mind, what would you like it to be?

Write down your ideas, hopes and dreams for your Mind's development and evolution.

How could your life be different if your mind really served your True Self?

Is your mind willing to be led and influenced by your spirit, and your highest calling?

Are you ready to make the changes necessary for your mind to grow into your truly loving, nurturing and supportive Big Self?

Meditation Three

Developing our Big Self

Settle down comfortably, and then take several deep breaths allowing you to draw in love and light with each in-breath and relax more and more deeply with each out-breath. Become aware of the back of the chair behind you, and imagine the chair becoming large and soft and supportive, holding you in a way that makes you feel safe and secure.

This might remind you of being a child, held safely while you relaxed in a parent's or grandparent's loving arms. If you never experienced this, don't worry….imagination is just as effective as memory, in conjuring up a totally nurturing experience. Allow yourself to feel small but safe, vulnerable but protected, totally receptive and appreciative of this unconditional loving presence that is supporting you. Realise you are literally being held in the arms of a Loving Universe.

You could imagine what this presence looks like, or you can simply be content to experience this sense of total acceptance, of unconditional love, of lifelong nurturing and support, of caring, understanding and devotion…….maybe for the first time in your life. Just bask in this loving presence, knowing you are a greatly loved child of the Universe.

So with this experience of God-given Divine Mother love let's turn to our feeling nature. What is her message to your feelings? …….Give yourself time to really sink deeply into this experience. Allow your sometimes difficult feeling nature to feel totally accepted, nurtured, loved and healed by your Inner Divine Mother.

And now what is her message to your Mind? Allow your mind to feel nurtured, loved and healed by your Inner Divine Mother. How can this presence slowly start to take over your mind? ….Can you imagine your Mind beginning to develop these same traits of unconditional love and acceptance, growing in to a truly wise and loving Big Self? Relax in this beautiful healing space, allowing this possibility to become a reality.

Chapter Four

BODY I: Whole Body Consciousness

In this chapter we are asking the question "How do we bring our consciousness right down into our body?"

Firstly, by becoming aware of our breathing in each moment (and not just when we are meditating, doing yoga or any other centring exercise). So many of us have learnt how to breathe deeply into our body, as a form of relaxation, but if we truly wish to develop a "Whole Body Awareness" we need to start noticing, at least every hour, if not every minute, "How are we breathing?"

Can you stop reading for a moment and put one hand on your belly and one on your upper chest. Just breathe as you normally would but start to watch closely how your hands are moving. Which hand is moving the most? Are you breathing from your belly or your chest? If the answer is shallowly, and up into the top part of your chest with the higher hand moving, but the lower one hardly at all, then you need to realise it is time to re-educate yourself as to a more healthy way to breathe.

However the first thing we need to do is offer ourselves love and acceptance for exactly what we are experiencing right now. We do not sink into Whole Body Consciousness by berating ourselves for where we are now. The object is to merely become the Witness, be the gentle Observer, and notice how we are breathing. Because full body breathing is our natural birth-right, it is how babies breathe; it is how my wonderful black cat is breathing as he lies curled up next to me on the settee as I write! So in becoming aware of our breathing and gently watching it with a loving, accepting gaze, it will naturally start to slow down and deepen, because that is our body being in its natural state, its place of rest.

Our aim is to breathe mainly from our diaphragm, the strong muscle that divides our lungs from our abdomen. It is known as diaphragmatic breathing and it means that when we watch our lower hand, we see it is moving out as our lungs inhale, and in as our lungs exhale. However the hand on our upper chest remains almost still, implying our breath is deep and slow and relaxed.

As we sink down into Whole Body Consciousness, we move away from the “Fight/Flight” reactions of the Sympathetic Nervous System, into the Para-Sympathetic Nervous System. This is the part of the autonomic nervous system that is responsible for the 'rest and digest' phase of the body. It governs activities that occur when the body is at rest, especially after eating. This enables us to leave behind the consciousness that keeps us in a state of incessant thoughts and worries as we relax down into a sense of “I am safe. All is well in my world”.

Do not be tempted to presume that if our body is in a state of rest and relaxation that our minds will switch off, and we will stop behaving in an efficient, functional manner. The reverse is actually true! When we give our bodies permission to relax and our awareness sinks down into our bellies, we become more centred, more calm, more truly aware and awake to our surroundings and circumstances. We find that we are more able to tap into our natural intuition, which will enable us to say and do exactly the right thing at the right time.

I first became aware of this when I worked as a professional therapist, in a busy NHS Community Mental Health Team. As I walked alone into the home of a mentally disturbed person, I intuitively knew that if I could remain aware of my own body and my own breathing I would emanate a sense of calm and poise and receptivity, which would enable them to slowly calm down, and unconsciously start to emulate me. Had I gone in to their home, reflecting back to them a sense of tension, fear, hostility or disapproval, they would have picked up on my feelings, which would only have escalated their own stress and anxiety.

It was several years after I retired from this work before I realised I was more anxious than I used to be, and it dawned on me that because I no longer worked in such a stressful environment I was no longer spending most of my day in a state of calm and relaxed breathing! So I have now taught myself how to breathe slowly and deeply from my belly, even when there is no pressing need for me to do this, as the world around me is perfectly comfortable, relaxed and happy.

Secondly, we deepen into Whole Body Consciousness by releasing past traumas. In the past when anything stressful happened in our lives, we were invariably unable to express the difficult feelings that we were experiencing, so we took this energy and unconsciously locked it away in our bodies…… and it remains there, locked in our cellular memory until we become both aware enough and safe enough to be able to release it. The body has a two-way transmission. It takes information in and it lets information out.

So when we experience tensions and uncomfortable sensations and we are able to ask our body "What is this sensation telling me? What is it reminding me of?" our body will release the memory of the time when we first locked away this negative energy. The only slight complication is, there may be several layers to this. We may have done an action-replay of the original difficulty on many occasions throughout our life, and may need help in unravelling the stress.

What is our BQ?

We all know about IQ (Intelligent Quotient), and many of us know a little about EQ (Emotional Intelligence Quotient). So now we need to ask ourselves "What is my Body's Intelligence Quotient? What is my relationship with my Body? What is my BQ? Am I seeing my body as my ally, or am I calling it names, judging it and constantly criticising it? Am I so disconnected to my body that I don't even know what my relationship is with it?"

For a moment, just go inside and ask yourself these questions. Are you surprised by your answer? Maybe you could pause and write in your journal your initial responses to these questions.

My teacher Steve Sisgold[4] suggests we heal our relationship with our body to the point where we can say at any hour of the day or night "Heh! My body rocks!" So even when we are tired or feeling unwell, we are still able to honour our body for the work it has done that has brought on this tiredness or unwell feeling. When we are able to thank and appreciate how well our body has functioned all these years, and accept it is not a machine, and it does need repeated rest, nourishing food, exercise and comfort, then we will start to feel a little better, even if we are still exhausted.

Then we need to look at how and why we disconnect from our bodies. Often when we are feeling uncomfortable, depressed or in a bad mood in order to self-medicate we turn on the TV, overeat or drink, engage in inauthentic laughter and false jollity or chatter endlessly to friends on the phone.... or anything to stop ourselves from feeling! However in so doing, instead of getting in to our body and asking it what is happening that is making us feel so uncomfortable, we do the opposite... we get out of the body!

What is your mechanism for masking what you are really feeling? Again take a moment to look at your current behaviour, and ask yourself if this behaviour continues to serve you. And if not, then perhaps you may be willing to attempt to do the Focusing Exercise[5] that follows, when you are feeling out of sorts, or something is bothering you.

One distinct advantage in doing a Focusing exercise instead of blanking off is that instead of dis-connecting with your body when you are experiencing difficult feelings, working with the “Felt-Sense” in this way actually brings you back into connection with your body. What we mean by the term “felt-sense”, is the sensations and tangible physical sense that seems to emanate from your body, rather than the thoughts and reactions you may have to the felt-sense.

The more you are willing to drop the mechanism of either blaming your body when you feel uncomfortable, or cutting off from it, the lighter your Body starts to feel. As we are able to stay in touch with our Whole Body Consciousness, with the sense of safety, trust and love that is our birth-right, we become more willing to stay with the difficult sensations as they arise, and are then led to the memory that needs healing.

Exercise Four
Focusing Exercise

When you find yourself feeling out-of-sorts for any reason, over-emotional, irritated or even suddenly quite devastated you may be sure a hidden part of yourself is coming up for air and needs to be focused on, in order to be released and healed. This exercise is adapted from the work of the American psychotherapist, Eugene T. Gendlin, and his book "Focusing"[6].

It is good if you write this in your journal, having divided the page into two columns. This is a dialogue between you and the part of you that is suffering. There are 8 questions which you ask the suffering part, allowing time for that part to answer truthfully. Do not go up into your head and tell yourself the answer, but remain in the "felt-sense" within your body, allowing an answer to arise spontaneously.

Having got an answer, then say out-loud "Hello" to the suffering part, thus involving it in the dialogue. I use an example I did a while ago when feeling disturbed.

You	***Suffering Self***
So how do you feel from your point of view?	*disturbed uncomfortable*

Hello Disturbed, Uncomfortable Self!

What is the Felt Sense

in your body?	*a bit sick and nauseous*
What is going on in your life that has prompted this feeling, or uncomfortable experience?	*A family issue*
What is happening that is bothering you the most?	*It is making me feel useless*
What is that reminding you of?	*It is reminding me of the time….*
What are you afraid of?	*Feeling powerless*
What do you need now?	*To stop feeling powerless*
*What do you **really** need from me right now?*	*To know I can now get help*

*I always find this exercise to be so effective because from the moment you say out loud "Hello……………Self", you are removing yourself from **being** your disturbed (or whatever your word is) self, and are once more the observer or witness. So even before you complete the exercise you are starting to feel better because you are now having a chat **with** the suffering part of you, but are no longer **identified with it.***

*By the time you get to the end of this exercise, the aspect of you that was suffering, already feels heard and understood so is able to recognise what its **true** needs are. Also having asked the questions **as** your True Self you have now re-identified with your strong* *adult self and are now feeling empowered and able to offer your small ego self the reassurance, love and support it needs to relinquish its hold over you.*

So breathe down into your belly, and begin to relax for a few breaths. Then coming from the most centred place you can find, ask yourself this question, "So how do you feel from your point of view?" then go quiet and allow your hurting self to answer you. Try and come up with just one or two words that describe how you are feeling about this issue. Then write out your own version of the exercise in your journal.

Meditation Four

Whole Body Consciousness Meditation

Take a few deep breaths, and begin to relax your **BODY**. Starting with your toes, begin to concentrate on each part of your body in turn. Firstly as you breathe in become aware of your toes, then as you breathe out, let go of any tension in your toes and allow that part of the body to relax. Working up through your feet, ankles, calves, knees, thighs, buttocks, back, lower body, stomach area, chest , hands, arms, shoulders, neck, head and scalp, and so totally relaxing your entire body.

Then think about your thoughts and your **MIND**. Start to become aware of your thoughts, watch them come into your field of awareness then watch them leave. Attempt to become an objective observer of your thoughts in this moment. So instead of actually getting caught up in your thoughts and running with them, for a while watch your thoughts come and go, just as if they were objects arising on a video screen.

Then think about your **FEELINGS**. Become aware of any emotion you are experiencing, and just like in the earlier part of the exercise, attempt to become an impartial observer of your feelings. Don’t get caught up in the highs or lows of your emotions, just witness what it is you are feeling. So name whatever feeling it is you are experiencing then just breathe it out, just as you did with the tension in your body….

Now, remaining deeply relaxed, but fully awake and conscious think of something you would really like to manifest in your life……. Then ask your Body what it thinks about that. What do you feel in your body when you visualise that happening in your life? Just allow yourself to feel into this felt sense with no sense of preference, judgement or criticism, just be open to what your body actually feels, with a sense of awe and wonder at the innate wisdom of your body.

If your body reacts positively, just allow yourself to picture this actually coming to fruition and be open to any messages your body wants to give you about actually what you need to do, if anything to bring this about…. and ignore the rest of what I am saying.

However if your body gives a negative reaction to the question, you can ask your body why doesn't it want you to manifest this? ………

What is the cellular memory that is being held in the body that is blocking you attracting this into your life? …….

I don't suggest you go deeply into this right now, just look at what it is and then promise yourself you will go into this when you can work one to one with someone who can guide you through this process. Honour what you see, feel, hear or experience, and continue to breathe slowly and deeply, as you send love and healing energy to this cellular memory……..Then slowly reconnect with your body, mind and feelings and come out of the meditation. Write down what you experienced in your journal.

Chapter Five

FEELINGS: Making friends with our feelings

In this chapter we are concentrating on getting to know and understand our FEELINGS, which for many people can often be a place they really don't want to go, experiencing themselves as having a damaged and often fragmented feeling nature. However if we return to the model of "The Mask, The Shadow and the True Self" discussed in Chapter 2, we can remind ourselves that our sometimes difficult and painful feelings do not represent the truth of who we REALLY are, merely a part of our Shadow Self that we need to move through on our journey from our Mask Self (the way we want others to see us) to our True Self.

So continuing on our journey of "Becoming Whole" and working our way clockwise around our "Wholistic Map", we can see that this area of feelings is truly our next destination. And it doesn't have to be as difficult a stop-over as we may have imagined. Feelings only really have a bad press because we live in a patriarchal society, where male dominated traits like mind, thinking, logic, knowledge, doing and power take precedent over more feminine traits such as feelings, heart, experience, being, caring, knowing and intuition. So for a moment, just imagine if we lived in a more balanced world we would not fear or wish to supress our feelings. Instead we would welcome them as our friends and allies, which is what they actually are.

So let's start this process by asking ourselves "What is my current relationship with my feeling nature or emotional self? Do I like my feelings? Do I trust them? Are they my best friend, and a trusted ally? Or do I feel they are out of control, confusing, frustrating or irrational?" Maybe pause for a moment and write down in your journal the answers to these questions.

Now for a moment imagine how different our feelings would be if they were constantly being reassured by a loving and understanding Mind or Big Self who in turn was working closely with our unconditionally loving Spirit. What if our Emotional Self wasn't constantly being silenced or worse still beaten up by our Judgemental Mind? What if our small frightened self, felt a constant warm and nurturing arm around its shoulders, reassuring it, listening to its woes, counselling it gently with words of reassurance, protection and love?

What if there was an understanding of where these insecure, powerless and sometimes irrational feelings came from, and a gentle reminder that they come from a previous time when we indeed **were** insecure and powerless. So they are not irrational, but perfectly understandable given the experiences we had at a younger age, when we couldn't make head nor tail of what was going on, and so of course reacted with fear, trepidation, anger, frustration and a sense of victimhood.

As we move through this book we will realise that the above description is not an improbable fantasy but an actual Cosmic Truth. In the next chapter we will look at our Spirit and some truths known to the sages of old, described in depth in all Ancient Wisdom Schools. When we begin to integrate these truths in to our lives we can begin to feel ourselves floating in a warm sea of love and caring. We can develop a sense of being connected to a good and loving universe that has our best interests at heart.

When we are feeling hurt, upset, angry, misunderstood, frightened or insecure in any way we often behave in ways that we later regret, or in ways that we now know are not representative of our True Self. So think back over the last few weeks to a time when you acted in a way that now makes you feel uncomfortable. When-ever we behave in ways that make us feel uncomfortable you can be certain there is a negative and unconscious emotional reaction going on. In what way did your emotions flood out in an unhealthy way? Do you now feel ready to work with and change this? What is the feeling associated with this behaviour and where in your body do you feel it?

There is a name that I give to this Shadow part of ourselves that often acts in ways we wish it didn't and feels things we don't want to feel. I call it "Little Self" and compared to our more rational, kind and loving self it is "little". It emanates from a time when we indeed were little, and totally ill-equipped to cope with some of the problems life was throwing at us.

For a moment think back to the behaviour that you just looked at and as you analyse how you were behaving you can allow yourself to remember the first time you behaved like that. The chances are you were quite small and it was actually totally appropriate behaviour for a small child of that age. However in the current context of adulthood it is probably inappropriate behaviour.

But instead of judging it now and condemning yourself for your apparently irrational behaviour you can start to realise it isn't irrational at all. When you first behaved like that as a child, you didn't have the resources and awareness that you now have all these years later. That truly was the best you could do at the time, from your limited awareness and understanding of the bigger picture. To you, the adults were behaving badly and you didn't understand why, so you reacted the way you did.

Looking at it with hindsight you understand why as a child you felt like you did and reacted the way you reacted back then. You can begin to see what was happening at that time in your life for you to forge the opinions and come to the conclusions you did. They were logical conclusions to draw given the circumstances. However it's important to realise that the circumstances of your life have changed. You no longer have to exist in such a difficult environment. You are now big and strong, capable and talented, connected to your Big Self, whom you met in Chapter 3. You now know you are held in the arms of a loving, caring Universe and are now able to make different choices, based on your new awareness. So coming from this new view of the world you are able to act differently, behaving in more aware and creative ways towards life's current ups and downs.

Exercise Five
Healing Little Self

In working with this exercise answer the questions and complete the statements in Part A totally from Little Self's perspective. Do not feel embarrassed by what emerges or try to change it by letting your mind intervene with more "acceptable" answers. Only by allowing Little Self to be totally honest about how it really experiences life, will you have the tools necessary for healing this damaged and stuck part of yourself.

Part A

What behaviour would you like to change?

And what is the feeling associated with that behaviour?

When I am thinking, feeling and behaving like that I believe

Life is ....
I am ....
Others are ....

How do I respond to life from this limited world view? Describe this behaviour pattern in minute detail, looking at each step in the order it presents itself.

First I.......
Later I ....
Then I .....
Finally I....

When you are thinking, feeling and behaving like this, about how old do you feel? And where in your body do you experience this feeling?

Part B

Now get up and move around, shrugging off this "Little Self" with its feelings and world view, realising it belongs to a past time, when life really did look like that from Little Self' s limited perspective. Re-connect with the kindest, most aware, loving, understanding Biggest Self you can imagine yourself to be. This Big Self has access to resources and strengths not available to your Little Self.

Describe how you felt and behaved when you last felt fully alive, energised and joyful. When you are experiencing this state, you are actually in contact with a much wider and more powerful energy field, and are in fact connected to universal energy. This is known as your Essence, your True Self. Where in the Body do you feel your Essence?

Your Essence knows the wisdom in becoming healed and whole, and knows we cannot truly move forward in life and fulfil our destiny until we DO embrace and nurture Little Self. Allow yourself to really feel genuine love, acceptance, and caring for Little Self and start to breathe love and healing to it. Take a look at the 3 statements made about "Life is…I am…..Others are…" from Little Self's limited perspective.

What is Big Self's answers to these statements? Tell the truth to your younger self from the deepest part of yourself. Help her to access a deeper truth than the one she has been trapped in, powerfully challenging the meanings and false conclusions she has drawn for so many years. Complete these definitions from a wiser perspective, writing down your new findings.

Life is ....

I am ....

Others are .... ..

Then return to your list of behaviours and write down "How do I respond to life from this altered world view? What are the new attitudes and behaviour patterns that I can start to adopt?" Start with the same statement or trigger that started the original process.

First I ....

Later I .....

Then I .....

Finally I……..

Now write a letter from Big Self to Little Self explaining that you understand why she feels like she does and reacts the way she reacts. Explain to her, what was happening at that time in her life for her to forge the opinions and come to the conclusions she has. They were logical conclusions to draw given the circumstances.

However remind her that the circumstances of her life have changed. She no longer has to exist in such a difficult environment. She is now big and strong, capable and talented, connected to her Big Self. She is held in the arms of a loving, caring Universe and is now able to make different choices, based on her new awareness. So coming from this new view of the world she is able to act differently, behaving in more aware and creative ways towards life's ups and downs.

Create and write out a Healing Statement, just a short phrase or sentence that explains your new understanding, and put it somewhere prominent in your home, as a constant reminder. At regular intervals throughout the day, check in to see where your energy centre is in that moment. If it has slipped back to Little Self, lovingly and gently suggest to yourself that you reconnect with your Big Self. Always be gentle and caring with yourself. Give yourself the love and understanding that was most likely not available to you when Little Self and her opinions were first formed. Enjoy and celebrate your new connection with Big Self!

I wish to thank Claire Zammit and Kathryn Woodward Thomas for their on-line Feminine Power Training, where I first came across a version of this exercise[7].

Meditation Five

Healing Little Self

Take a few deep breaths, and begin to relax your **BODY**. Starting with your toes, begin to concentrate on each part of your body in turn. Firstly as you breathe in become aware of your toes, then as you breathe out let go of tension in your toes, and allowing that part of the body to relax. Working up through your feet, ankles, calves, knees, thighs, buttocks, back, lower body, stomach area, chest , hands, arms, shoulders, neck, head and scalp, and so totally relaxing your entire body.

Then think about your thoughts and your **MIND**. Start to become aware of your thoughts, watch them come into your field of awareness then watch them leave. Attempt to become an objective observer of your thoughts in this moment. So instead of actually getting caught up in your thoughts and running with them, for a while watch your thoughts come and go, just as if they were objects arising on a video screen.

Then think about your **FEELINGS**. Become aware of any emotion you are experiencing, and just like in the earlier part of the exercise, attempt to become an impartial observer of your feelings. Don't get caught up in the highs or lows of your emotions, just witness what it is you are feeling. So name whatever feeling it is you are experiencing then just breathe it out, just as you did with the tension in your body.

Now, remaining deeply relaxed, but fully awake and conscious feel the place in your Body you now know to be your Essence or your new Big Self. Then become conscious of the place where Little Self lives. Allow unconditional love and healing to start to flow from one to the other. Physically feel a current of warm air circulating round your body bringing acceptance and healing to your emotional body.

Allow Big Self to start to explain to Little Self that you understand why it feels the way it feels and reacts the way it reacts. Explain to it, what was happening at that time in your life for Little Self to forge the opinions and come to the conclusions it has. Remind yourself that they were logical conclusions to draw given the circumstances.

However remind Little Self that the circumstances of its life have now changed. Little Self no longer has to exist in such a difficult environment.

Little Self has now grown up!

Little Self is now big and strong, capable and talented, connected to your Essence.

Little Self is held in the arms of a loving, caring Universe and is now able to make different choices, based on a new awareness.

So coming from this new view of the world Little Self is able to act differently, behaving in more aware and creative ways towards life's ups and downs.

Complete the following statements, and then end the meditation by writing up your experience in your journal.

As Big Self I now see……………

Also I now understand…………..

And I now realise……………..

Chapter Six

SPIRIT: Mindfulness

We are now going to be looking at SPIRIT, and how to actually EMBODY Spirit. So just as in chapter 4 we looked at how to BE IN our bodies, in this chapter we are looking at how to BE IN our Spirit, not just talking ABOUT Spirit! So many books teach us ABOUT spirituality, but my aim here is to get us to DIRECTLY EXPERIENCE our own spirituality.

It may be helpful here to again look back at the second part of the Wholistic Map model we worked with in Chapter 2. In that chapter we imagined our personality to be made up of 3 layers, a little like Russian Dolls, each layer inside the other. The outer one represented "The Face we Show to the World" OR OUR Mask Self, the middle one was "The Face we hide from the world" or our Shadow Self, and the inside one was "The Face of WHO WE TRULY ARE" or our True Self, which may not be a face we know very well at all! Perhaps if we are a meditator we are able to reach this space during a good meditation, but few of us are able to consistently be this Self at will.

So right now we are not concentrating on the two outer parts of ourselves, which actually represent someone we are not, that is neither our Mask Self nor yet our Shadow Self. But we are now going to spend time looking at who we ACTUALLY ARE!

But first, one important point to remember is that the image in Figure 3, in chapter 2 is actually three dimensional. As we go towards our centre, we start to move in an inner direction, leaving behind our separated ego and shadow selves, and in this centre we move through on to a different plane where we are at one with not only the Source, or Great Spirit or God/Goddess/All-That-Is (which ever name you feel most comfortable using) and our own True Self or Essence, but also we are at one with the True Self and Essence of each other.

This marks an amazingly important milestone on our journey to Wholeness. It is our outer self, which includes both our Mask and Shadow selves that has problems with our relationships with others. When we are able to move into the truth of ourselves, we are able to leave our egoic self behind, and start to consistently come from a place of truth, love, acceptance, harmony, beauty and peace. So how can we get to that stage of our development?

One way to help us connect more easily to our True Self or Spirit is through working with Mindfulness[8].

Mindfulness originated as an ancient art of mind control practised by the Buddhist monks of Tibet and Thailand for thousands of years. However over the last 30 years Jon Kabat-Zinn, a psychotherapist from the University of Massachusetts Medical Centre and his colleagues developed a group programme, based on the same principles, for people suffering from both mental and physical health problems which they called Mindfulness-based Stress Reduction.

This programme teaches its clients how to overcome extreme levels of stress caused by either prolonged and severe physical pain, or debilitating levels of anxiety or depression by becoming mindful or aware of whatever is happening in their experience moment to moment. By paying deliberate attention to what is going on in their mind, body, feelings and experience, totally without judgement or self-criticism, these clients have found unexpected benefits.

Most of us find that by sitting quietly and monitoring what is actually going on, rather than focusing on what we fear **might** go on in the future, we are able to reduce our stress levels. Also this quiet contemplative attitude often allows new positive ideas about how to handle the problem to surface, and be thought about, instead of the tired old habitual response that was there in the past. New inner strengths and unexpected avenues of help are also more likely to present themselves to a quiet mind than a racing, stressed one.

As long as we are thinking about wanting things to be different, we are not looking at what is actually good in our lives at this moment. We all know the old maxim "What we resist persists." Also it is important to discuss here the concept that we create our own reality. What does this actually mean? It means that whatever we concentrate on, will magnify itself and become even truer for us. So if we are spending a lot of time thinking about all the dreadful things that have happened to us in the past, we are more likely to attract more of the same.

Anthony Robbins said "If we always do what we've always done, we'll always get what we've always got" However if we are able to stop focusing on the past, and instead learn through giving Mindful Attention to our thoughts they will automatically start to change to something more positive, up-lifting and helpful. And then we will most definitely start to manifest something more positive in our life.

And what is wonderful about learning Mindfulness is the fact that we do not need to spend hours re-telling our sad stories to a therapist, at enormous monetary cost, plus great emotional cost to ourselves, by reliving the past as we recount it. Mindfulness is more to do with training ourselves how to do a daily practice which gives us a new skill and a new approach to life, rather than a therapy to be administered by the therapist to the client.

The programme, started in America, has now spread to many other countries including England and Wales. The Centre for Mindfulness at Bangor University runs courses where therapists can train, and now it is possible to request to join a Mindfulness-based group on the NHS. Mindfulness-based approaches teach practical skills that are designed to help with daily challenges due to many health problems. Although the idea originated from Buddhism, nowadays it is taught in a totally non-religious context.

The core skill of Mindfulness is to change gear. So instead of focusing on the repeated negative patterns, the focus is on becoming more aware of physical sensations, thoughts and feelings as simple mental events as they occur moment to moment. When seen in this way, it is possible to notice the transient nature of thoughts, feelings and sensations. Left to their own devices these experiences come and go, but are not cast in stone. It is only our attitude to them that can remain fixed and therefore falsely cement them in place.

The aim of Mindfulness is not actually to stop the negative thinking, merely to become aware of it and watch it calmly without judgement until it moves into something else.

By working in this way, it allows us to have a healthier relationship to thoughts, feelings and sensations. We can see them as aspects of our experience, which are moving through our awareness in the moment. They are not our total reality. In other words, "I have these thoughts, feelings and sensations, but I am actually more than just them. I am an Aware Self, which is able to watch these experiences come and go", which is what we learnt in the first meditation in this book.

The way this works is very similar to the experience of feeling better after having shared a negative experience with a friend. When we are thinking about it afterwards we cannot remember what the friend actually said, but what we do know is we feel better for having shared the experience. When we bring a Mindful approach to bear on a problem we are experiencing, we actually are doing the same thing. We are sharing our difficult experience with our True Self, and as such end up feeling better, even though the outer problem hasn't changed.

We feel better because our awareness is what has changed. We are no longer IDENTIFYING with the problem for example "I am very upset", but are identified with our wise True Self. Its stance may be "It is very sad that this has happened, but I am able to breathe deeply, relax and let go of these strong feelings. I am stronger than I realised and as my True Self I am able to cope with this and in time these overwhelming feelings will indeed pass".

Exercise Six

Mindfulness Exercise

Sit in a comfortable position, preferably in a straight backed chair, with your feet on the floor.

Concentrate on your breathing. Don't try to change it at all, just become aware of watching yourself breath in and out. Watch the speed, the depth and the quality of each breath, noting the space between the breaths too. Notice any changes that naturally occur in the breathing pattern as you watch it.........

Now concentrate on your bodily sensations. What part of your body is drawing your attention? Is that because it is uncomfortable? Ask yourself what sort of discomfort is this? Describe the sensations to yourself..........

Breathe into the sensations in a calm relaxed way. Just let them be. Even if somewhere is quite painful, note it is painful but without a value judgment, just breathe into the pain. As the sensations change, notice the change and continue to breathe.....

Become aware of your thoughts. Just watch them come and go in the same detached way you have just been experiencing your physical sensations. Realise that, like the sensations, they come and go. Become aware of not taking too much notice of each individual thought, believing it is the absolute truth........

Understand our thoughts are just streams of consciousness, some sensible, some not! We don't need to listen to them all. Just watch them drift into and out of your mind, and start to become aware of the transient nature of thought. Reconnect to your breathing in a relaxed, calm way as you watch your thoughts come and go……..

Now become aware of your feelings, watching them come and go in the same relaxed, detached way. If a feeling is particularly strong, breathe into the strong feeling, just allowing it to be how it is, with no judgment or criticism. Watch how it changes as you observe it………

Return to concentrating on your breathing and when you are ready,

slowly stretch and yawn and return to being here now. Note any difference in your overall sense of well-being………

The more you do this exercise the easier it becomes and the more benefit you will get out of it. The key to its success is to be gentle with yourself, not berating yourself when your mind wanders, just gently bringing your mind back to the point, aware that you wandered off for a while. If you do it regularly, when you are really stressed or in pain you will find it is able to considerably reduce your stress levels, and improve your ability to cope in your day to day life.

Meditation Six

Turning on the Inner Light Bulb

Settle down in a comfortable place where you can see both some foreground and also the sky out of a window. This is a very simple practice that helps you to connect with the Light that always shines inside yourself.

There is no right or wrong way to do this, whatever happens is fine. There are no rules in this process, just a sense of allowing everything to be just as it is right now.

Allow your eyes to rest on a point near the horizon. Describe to yourself what you can see, maybe trees, hills or buildings.

Now let each part of this view represent a part of your being. Let the closest or largest tree or building represent your body; another one can represent your mind; and another one can represent your feelings. All these objects you are looking at may be mainly static as in the hill or building or they may be changing rapidly like a bird flying across the sky or the wind ruffling the leaves on a tree.

Begin to realise that the one thing all these objects in the foreground have in common is the fact that they do not last for ever. All things in the foreground are changing and ephemeral to some extent. Even a building will one day be demolished and the hill was once, thousands of years ago, a different shape and size.

Now connect to the shifting nature of your Body's sensations. If you have any pain or tension in the body, breathe into it, and as you breathe out, allow the pain or tension to be released with the out breath.

Next connect to the shifting nature of your thoughts, feelings and behaviour patterns, and again breathe into these patterns then be willing to suspend them for the duration of this meditation and release them as you breathe out. They too come and go and start to change over time. Nothing of this outer "you" is fixed for ever.

Now return to your view out of the window and slowly become aware of "The Bigger Picture". What is behind the trees, hills or buildings that you are looking at? Yes the sky is always behind whatever we look at, it always has been and always will be. The sky is always in the background, a constant, unchanging anchor.

So now let the sky in the background represents your spirit, your connection with the whole. And as you rest your gaze on the background and the sky, you realise it remains the same, whether the trees, buildings or hills are there or are not there.

The background is unaffected by the foreground. Even if clouds are present, you know the blue sky constantly exists unchanging behind them. Deeply connect to the unchanging quality of the blue sky. Behind all the comings and goings of clouds, birds, trees in the foreground, the blue sky remains constant, never changing, everlasting, stretching out to infinity in all directions.

Feel yourself sinking down into this part of yourself that is also never changing, constant, steady, at peace, calm and serene just like the blue sky. Become aware of the context in which all the foreground phenomena happen. There is a backdrop, a vast empty space in which thoughts and feelings and sensations arise. Slowly become even more aware of this space, this vast empty space and realise it doesn't matter if thoughts, sensations and feelings are there or not there.

Their presence doesn't change the peaceful nature of this space. They come and go but this space remains the same. If it feels comfortable allow your eyes to close in order to sink down more deeply into this place. However if you feel resistant to doing this, that is fine. Just continue to focus on the sky with a relaxed softly focused gaze.

This space can be seen as consciousness or awareness. It remains untouched by anything that happens within it. This is your spiritual power! Just allow everything to be just as it is right now. Allow yourself to become totally content with what is, with no need to change anything at all.

Deeply connect with your Spiritual Power, which sees the Bigger Picture. It has no needs or wants, no lack or absence of anything. Your Spirit is already connected to the Whole Universe. It needs nothing. Allow yourself to sink down into this place that is outside of time, the place that has never been part of time and change. It is timeless and changeless.

This has been called The Ground of Being, Consciousness Itself or Spirit. Allow this Consciousness to ignite your Inner Light Bulb. Allow it to turn on your Inner Light Bulb! Allow yourself to wake up to this Connection with Source, Great Spirit or God/Goddess/All That Is.

While you are resting in this timeless place, try to describe to yourself what you are experiencing in this space. However try to do this without leaving this place or going up into your head to find words. Your Spirit has its own language and words, so try to listen for them to arise....

From this place what are you aware of? What does it feel like to be here? Is there any information your Spirit wishes to tell you? Then when you feel ready allow this illumination, this glowing Light Bulb to begin to reconnect to the part of you that inhabits the foreground.

Allow this Light to start to shine on the objects in the foreground that represented your mind, body and feelings. Allow your Spiritual Light to shine Light, Love and a Deep Spiritual Connection on to them all, illuminating them from the inside. There are parts of you that desperately need your love, understanding and support. Realise they don't need to remain "in the dark" any longer!

So now allow your Spiritual Light to shine Light, Love and a Deep Spiritual Connection out in to the world, illuminating it from inside you, allowing transformation and healing to be radiated out worldwide, and even out into the Universe!

Open your eyes, and return to the room knowing you are constantly connected to Light, Love and your own Spirit.

Chapter Seven
MIND II: Changing Limiting Beliefs

In this chapter we are going to be again concentrating on MIND, just as we did in Chapter 3, but this time we are going to focus on one very important aspect of our cognitive thinking processes, our beliefs. What are Beliefs? According to the Concise Oxford Dictionary *"Beliefs: trust or confidence in; acceptance of thing, fact, statement as true or existing"*, so let's take a look at some of our beliefs and see if they really ARE true, actually existing, and something that we can definitely trust or have confidence in.

Have you ever thought just how important our beliefs are, how they define us as a person and what a deep influence our beliefs have over our lives? We are not talking here about our obviously influential beliefs such as religion or politics, which if we are relatively open minded can often change over time anyway. No, I'm talking about those apparently innocuous little beliefs, such as:-

> It's not my fault my life turned out the way it did
>
> I'm just an unlucky person
>
> I've never been a confident person
>
> There's never enough to go round, life is always a struggle
>
> I have to fight to get anywhere in life

I can't cope with not being liked

I have to always please others and do what they want me to do

At some stressful and formative moment in our history we made a decision about something and invariably have never reviewed that decision from that day to this. It becomes carved in stone, turning from a decision to a belief and from there, starts to define who we are, what our *take* on life is. Now it may have been absolutely true when we first said it to ourselves, but everything changes over time.

All things are relative, and what appears true from one angle, as we move, grow and change usually can be seen from other points of view as time passes. But unless we give ourselves time and space to periodically review and up-date our beliefs, we may become stuck in an out-dated version of ourselves. It is always much easier to see these unhelpful beliefs in someone other than ourselves. For a moment, stop and think of a friend or relative who seems to be stuck in either blame, victimhood, low self-esteem, or trauma.

What is the statement they repeatedly make about themselves or their life? Maybe you know enough about them and their history to know that statement is not completely factually true. Maybe it was true when they started saying it, but you know they are now repeating it like a stuck record, oblivious of the fact their circumstances are now different.

As humans we are incredibly good at only seeing what we want to see and blocking out from our awareness those situations that make us feel uncomfortable. And what is more uncomfortable than seeing or hearing something we really don't agree with? In general we hate having our beliefs threatened. But if we ask ourselves what is the worst of it, we will discover that it is the feeling of having been proved wrong, of having made a mistake. But surely it's better to recognise we have made a mistake, forgive ourselves and move on, rather than going on for the rest of our lives making the same mistakes over and over? We can re-define ourselves, and start behaving in ways we have not done before, if we so choose.

Just for a minute think of a negative belief we may have about a person we once knew. It is hardly surprising that if, when we were having a very hard time with someone in our past we justifiably formed a strong negative definition of them. So now, years later we may be still unwilling to see that maybe they are not so bad after all. We don't want to have to face the uncomfortable feeling that perhaps we were wrong about them. Maybe they aren't the totally negative person we made them out to be. "It takes two to tango" and it could be we were not being an angel ourselves at the time either! Perhaps we were both under stress, and neither of us was behaving like rational mature adults. It is no surprise that we choose to only see what we want to see, or hear only what we want to hear.

So if someone is telling us about how kind this person has been to a friend who was ill, we will dismiss their comments as being out of character, and then go on to put this piece of information out of our minds. However if someone had told us something bad this person had done, we would be more likely to get into a long discussion on all his shortcomings, and then add this new information to our already bulging arsenal against him! And why? Because the first one made us feel threatened and uncomfortable because our existing belief was challenged. The second one reinforced our already existing belief, making us feel justified and self- righteous.

If we believe that our background or even a traumatic incident or loss has ruined our life, and all our personal failings are a direct result of this happening to us, we don't want to be reminded that others in a similar position, did as the Fred Astaire's song suggests "pick yourself up, dust yourself off and start all over again!" It fits in with our beliefs to hold tightly to the victim stance. Being a victim definitely appears to have its benefits, until we realise the dreadful cost of maintaining this stance.

Firstly, by remaining a victim, we appear to have a wonderful reason not to have to take responsibility for what we are attracting to us. It can initially seem great when we can blame all our ills on someone or something else! It can at first make us feel sure of ourselves. The universe is known, understood. But at what cost to ourselves? Of course, we will not be put up for promotion, or attract happy, healthy people into our lives if we are constantly blaming other people for all our ills.

Also our beliefs tend to reinforce themselves, because the negative belief attracts more negativity to us for one simple reason. The universe reflects back to us what we tell ourselves about it! If we think it's a lovely benign place, quite often it will prove us right, by good things happening to us. If on the other hand we believe nothing we do ever works, nothing *will* ever work, because our belief is proving us right by only attracting negative situations and people to us.

We need to be able to see in our own mind that the belief is indeed limiting, and possibly even erroneous. So the following exercises will only help if you are already able to say that although you always used to believe it, you can now see it is not necessarily still true. What is more you are becoming aware of how this belief, plus the feelings that go with it are in fact holding you back and it is time to move on.

We are so much more powerful than we think we are! Our thoughts and beliefs carry the power to transform our reality. So select a negative belief that you would like to take into the next exercise with you. Can you think of one of your beliefs that once defined you, but now you are beginning to wonder if it really is true.

Exercise Seven
Beach Ball Exercise

Close your eyes and relax…….Now imagine you are sitting opposite a person with radically differing views on life from you, who believes something totally different from your beliefs. For example you may have been raised as a pacifist, while they are from a military background; or you are a vegetarian and they are a carnivore; or you believe in freedom of speech and they believe in press censorship. It doesn't matter what it is, just that it is different from yours.

Then imagine that between the two of you is a large beach ball, so large you cannot see the person you are sitting opposite. However you find yourself involved in an argument about the colour of the beach ball. You are insistent it is a blue ball, but your unseen protagonist is equally insistent it is in fact a red ball.

How can this issue ever be resolved?

Only when you become willing to leave your comfortable chair and known position and start to walk around the large obstacle, approaching your opponent and their position do you suddenly realise you are actually wrong. This is not a blue ball you are looking at, it is actually a two coloured ball, blue on your side and red on theirs!

Having made this enormous shift, two amazing things happen. Firstly in becoming willing to leave your entrenched position behind, you have freed up you chair, and there is a distinct possibility that now that position is free, your opponent may take up the option of also leaving their chair and equally entrenched position, and walking round the obstacle, finally seeing how it looks from your side!

And secondly as you both walk around, agreeing it is in fact a two coloured ball, as you look up, towards the top of the ball, you realise from a "God's Eye View", neither of you are right, because it is in fact a 3 colour ball, as from a Higher Perspective, it is actually purple, a wonderful blend of all perspectives!............

So now could you consider a belief you have held for a long time, which you would like to possibly consider changing. I will use an example from my own life. I had been raised as a pacifist, but in the course of my working life I once worked in an area of the country where most of my clients and their relatives were from a military background. In order to be able to truly connect deeply with my clients I needed to be willing to shift my perspective, away from being very against all forms of military intervention at least to a neutral perspective.

Now as you close your eyes and imagine the beach ball again you remember neither side has got a complete handle on the truth, so can you be prepared to give up on your original view and actually hear the opposite view and then look for a higher perspective?

If so, deeply relax and then imagine someone with a totally opposite view point to you is sitting on the other side of this large ball telling you why you are wrong in your views. Allow yourself to really hear this argument, maybe for the first time in your life, rather than just dismissing it out of hand. Listen and allow this view point to be seen as just as valid as your own. If you want to, imagine yourself getting up and walking around the ball, then sitting in their chair, really seeing how life looks when you sit in this chair with this view.

Then when you are ready to see they too have a valid viewpoint, it's time to imagine climbing up on a step ladder and viewing the ball from the top. So what could be a higher perspective, and nearer to God's Eye View or absolute truth? How do the two opposing views blend together into one more cohesive, fully comprehensive and beautiful new view?

Sit with this new awareness, then write it down in your journal.

Meditation Seven
Changing Beliefs Meditation

Take a few deep breaths, and begin to relax your **BODY**. Starting with your toes, begin to concentrate on each part of your body in turn. Firstly as you breathe in become aware of your toes, then as you breathe out let go of tension in your toes, and allowing that part of the body to relax. Working up through your feet, ankles, calves, knees, thighs, buttocks, back, lower body, stomach area, chest, hands, arms, shoulders, neck and head, and so totally relaxing your entire body.

Then think about your thoughts and your **MIND**. Start to become aware of your thoughts, watch them come into your field of awareness then watch them leave. Attempt to become an objective observer of your thoughts in this moment. So instead of actually getting caught up in your thoughts and running with them, for a while watch your thoughts come and go, just as if they were objects arising on a video screen.

Then think about your **FEELINGS**. Become aware of any emotion you are experiencing, and just like in the earlier part of the exercise, attempt to become an impartial observer of your feelings. Don't get caught up in the highs or lows of your emotions, just witness what it is you are feeling. So name whatever feeling it is you are experiencing then just breathe it out, just as you did with the tension in your body….

Now imagine that you are about to be going on a journey, a train journey. But as you attempt to board the train you are aware that you are carrying an enormous block of stone. You stagger on to the train, totally weighed down by the enormous weight of the burden that you are carrying.

As the train moves off you become aware that this heavy burden is your negative belief. It is a large concrete block. Become aware that the train is going in to a tunnel. The block is getting bigger and heavier. The lights are inadequate and you are aware of the darkness through which you are passing. This reminds you of the time when you first took on this negative belief. Feel the feelings associated with this negative belief. Name them! Think about the belief and your wish to be free of it.

Concentrate on your desire to leave behind this belief. As you do so, become aware of a tiny point of light at the end of the tunnel. Concentrate on going in to the light and leaving the darkness behind. Become aware of everything being in a state of flow, of movement. As the light increases begin to sense *"Nothing is concrete! Nothing is set in stone! Everything is fluid and mobile!"*

Look down at your block of concrete and begin to see it with new eyes. See the molecules dancing and moving inside it. See the waves and particles that make up the atoms in the stone as fluid, moving, constantly changing with space between them, alive, living, breathing.

Feel it, touch it, taste it…and realise it is sweet! Your block of concrete is actually a great big marshmallow!!

Now what is the sweetest, loveliest, most beautiful thing that your belief could change into? What belief could you choose to believe that would be most beneficial and helpful to you in your life right now?

Bring yourself back slowly and write down the original negative belief and what it changed into, as you journeyed with it.

Chapter Eight
BODY II – Developing Whole Person Actions

In chapter 3 we looked at how our Spirit is able to influence our Mind in order to evolve beyond our basic ego mind, by allowing Mind to embrace a feeling of God-given Mother love, known also as the Divine Feminine Principle, thus becoming an unconditionally loving support and healer to our fragmented Little Self.

In this chapter we are going to be looking at how our Spirit is able to equally influence our Body in order to evolve beyond our basic egoic relationship with it, by allowing Body to embrace the Divine Masculine Principle, thereby developing the ability to act or behave with integrity, consistency, power and success in the world. As we do this we are able to start contributing to the creation of a Whole World, and becoming God's hands and feet, or God in Action.

What is your current relationship with your Body? We looked at this question in Chapter 4 when we first studied Whole Body Consciousness. So now we are going to take an even deeper dive into our relationship with our Body to see if we can evolve it still further.

One of the first questions we can ask ourselves could be "Is my Body aligned to my mind or are they out of sync?" Does our body frequently have a different idea of our capabilities than our mind has? If this is the case, would it be helpful if our mind became willing to listen to, accept, respect and recognise what activities feel authentic and realistic for our

Body to be attempting, at the age we now are, and with the health challenges we may be facing. And which activities are best left to those with the kind of body that relishes those exercises and activities? We wouldn't push our 4 year old to accomplish what his 12 year old brother easily accomplishes, so why do we expect our 50 year old body to still behave as it did when we were aged 18?

In order to understand why we are often unnecessarily hard on our body, it may be advisable to imagine ourselves going right back to our very first experience of "being in a body". If you could actually remember, what would have been your first ever bodily experience when your mother first realised she was pregnant with you? What was the message coming from your parents into your tiny body? Yes, it could well be something of a shock to begin to wonder what false belief about your self was formulated in that moment.

And of course it didn't stop there. Can we start to consider how our body must have felt as a child or young teenager when we were mocked or teased for certain physical attributes, like our size, spots, poor hand-eye co-ordination or buck teeth. Can you tell where in your body you experienced this shame, embarrassment, or self-hatred? Of course if you have never asked yourself these kind of questions before, it may be your body is still holding those sensations close to its chest! Just pause for a moment and ask yourself "How does my body feel right now?"

It may be helpful to get out your journal and write down a description of your bodily sensations when you remember these earlier and formative experiences. What is important to realise is that you are not alone with these unpleasant feelings. When I taught this session in the first pilot Study Group, I was interested to note how all the students were experiencing very similar physical sensations and describing very similar feelings.

When you see this is part of the current human condition, you are more likely to be able to realise that in common with most other adults, these feelings and sensations belong to an earlier time in your development. Now is the time to let them go, as they no longer serve you. Nor do they represent the truth of your current life experience.

It is often helpful in order to heal and release these memories to ask yourself what sorts of situations trigger these same sensations now. And when you are triggered, how do these physical sensations influence your behaviour? As long as this process is unconscious we have little chance of evolving our reactions. However, once it becomes conscious we can start to have choices. It becomes easier to change as we understand the origin of these triggers and we can begin to make a conscious choice to respond rather than react to these triggers.

This is where our Spirit can influence our relationship with our Body. If you believe in the power of prayer, you could ask your Spirit for some help in releasing these painful memories, and letting go of unhelpful beliefs about your body. If prayer is not something you feel comfortable with, then just affirming that you are indeed held in the arms of a loving universe, and are grateful for finally seeing these negative and false beliefs will help to release these patterns.

The Divine Masculine Principle is the concept of opening to expressing right behaviour in the world. It is about Divine Doing. We are expressing the Divine Masculine when all our actions are in line with our highest truth, when we are consistently authentic and aware of our actions and the influence we have on the world through our actions.

Just as the Divine Feminine Principle helped us to heal our mind, when we embrace the concept of the Divine Masculine Principle, we are allowing our Spirit to influence how we behave, healing our relationship with our Body. We are then able to develop the ability to behave with integrity, consistency, power and success in the world, thus contributing to the creation of a Whole World, and becoming God's hands and feet or God in Action.

Exercise Eight
Healing our Relationship with our Body

If you haven't already done so, maybe put down the book and get out your journal. Write a little about how you felt about your body when you were a child or young adult. For most of us there was a phase in our development when we didn't think our body compared well with the bodies of our peers. So we may have started working out, or changed our diet and succeeded in changing our body image. But the million dollar question is, did we simultaneously change our perception of our body? Or did we continue to criticise it and feel embarrassed by it even after it grew into a perfectly reasonable body?

The more I have taught this concept the more surprised I am to find that often we unconsciously continue resenting and blaming our body merely out of habit, when actually if we were to realise how inappropriate that is, because our body is actually great, and functioning very well. In the last chapter we looked at beliefs that no longer serve us, or are in fact no longer even true, but we carry on believing them, simply because we always have believed them. So take time out to review your relationship with your body, and if you realise it's time to let go of some false beliefs about how you view your body, then re-do the exercise in the previous chapter.

Now, remembering the session we did on Big Self and Little Self, we did an exercise where we looked at life from Little Self's limited perspective, then changed into Big Self and reassured Little Self that we had now moved on. We are no longer stuck in that difficult position. We now have skills, awareness, support, love and encouragement that was probably not available to us then.

So now remembering yourself as the teenager who probably didn't like your body very much, can you complete the following sentence,

"When I am thinking, feeling and behaving like that, I believe….

Life is ....
I am ....
Others are .... .."

Now respond from the perspective of your Inner Divine Mother, that is with total acceptance, non-judgement and unconditional love, reassuring you that life has indeed changed for the better now. When you are feeling reassured, turn back to your writing, and update your self-belief.

"That was then, but this is now. Now I believe

Life is ....
I am ....
Others are .... .."

Allow yourself to really experience this shift in your consciousness from berating and blaming your body, to appreciating it, expressing gratitude to it, and starting to really enjoy having this wonderful unique body.

Meditation Eight

Healing our Relationship with our Body

Breathe into body, mind and feelings relaxing completely. Now, remaining deeply relaxed, but fully awake and conscious feel the place in your Body you now know to be your Essence or your new Big Self ….

Applying what you just learnt in Exercise 8, allow Big Self to start to explain to your Body that you understand why it feels the way it feels and reacts the way it reacts. Explain to it, what was happening at that time in your life for you to forge the opinions and come to the conclusions about your body that you did. They were logical conclusions to draw given the circumstances.

However, remind Body that the circumstances of its life have now changed. Body no longer has to exist in such a difficult environment. Body has now grown up!

You maybe didn't like Body very much back then both for how it sometimes felt or looked and because of the hurtful things others sometimes said about it. However Body is now big and strong, capable and talented, connected to your Essence. Body is always held in the arms of a loving, caring Universe and is now able to make different choices, based on a new awareness.

Big Self knows just how amazing Body is, and what a good job it does each day. So coming from this new view of the world you are able to feel differently and act differently, behaving in more aware and creative ways towards Body's various aches and pains or issues.

Allow a memory of gratitude for someone to emerge. Think of the circumstances where you felt gratitude for someone. Become aware of where in your body you are feeling this gratitude. Do you feel a warm glow in your heart when you think of this person or situation? Bask in this warm glow of gratitude.

Then allow the recipient of this gratitude to shift to your own body. Realise just how amazing your body is. Think about all the unconscious workings that go on 24/7 without you having to pay them any attention, like your digestion, your breathing, your heart and your circulation. Thank them and send love and gratitude to them all.

Then think about your skeletal system and your muscles. Marvel at how responsive they are to your bidding. Even if you have some problems your body is still totally miraculous. Thank them and send love and gratitude to all parts of your body.

Then think about the part of your body you like the least. Realise it is still a wonderful asset to you, and how much worse your life would be if you no longer had this part of your body. Thank it and send love and gratitude to the least favourite parts of your body.

Let a Body Gratitude Statement form in your mind then slowly come out of the meditation and write it down in your journal. By referring back to this statement regularly, it helps to reconnect you with this feeling of gratitude for your body.

So now you can see how your Spirit is able to influence your Body in order to evolve beyond Ego, by allowing Body to embrace the Divine Masculine Principle. And as it does so you are able to develop the ability to act or behave with integrity, consistency, power and success in the world, thus contributing to the creation of a Whole World, becoming God's hands and feet, or God in Action.

Come out of this meditation and write what you experienced in your journal.

Chapter Nine

Completing the Spiral of Wholeness

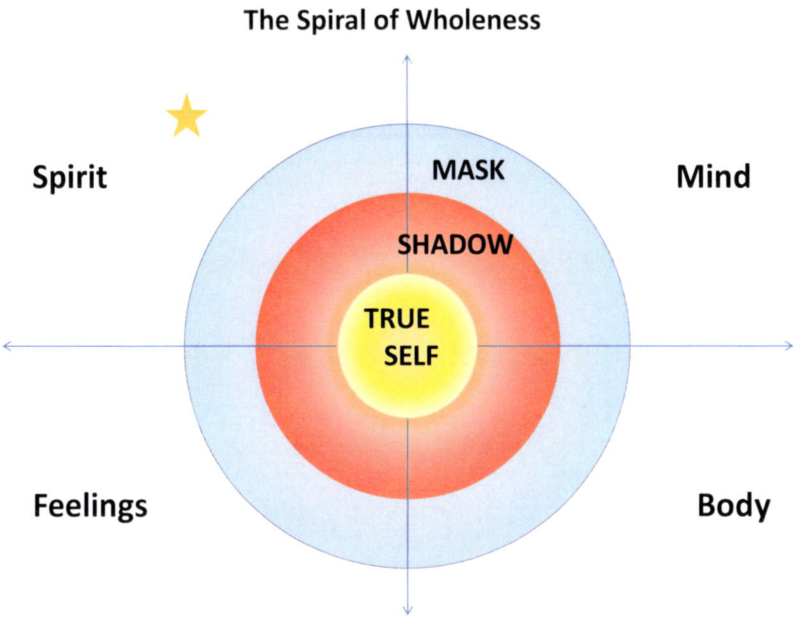

Fig. 4

Can you look for a moment at Figure 4. As you can see this is a combination of Figures 1 and 2, which is actually a combination of the two parts of the Wholistic Map, incorporating the model of " The Mask, The Shadow and The True Self" described in chapters one and two.

Imagine that when we are first born, when we first come in to incarnation, we arrive into the centre of our Wholistic Map. We arrive whole and perfect, as in the concept of Primal Spirituality as described earlier. The old Christian teaching that we are "born in sin", is not only a lie, but a dangerous and damaging belief, originating in the dark ages, and totally out of keeping with the true words of the originator of the Christian faith.

It was only ever introduced in order to disempower and terrorise the people, so they would pay money to the priests to have their souls saved. However the truth is we come in with perfect souls, in need of no-one to act as intermediators between ourselves and the Source, in need of no-one to save us.

But despite being born into perfection, once we find ourselves in the dense and often negative vibration that exists on the earth plane, we move out of the centre, often during early childhood, losing our conscious connection with the Source. Then as we grow and develop throughout our childhood and adolescence, due to our conditioning, we tend to further distance ourselves from our original positive mind set by continuing to spiral outwards and downwards, often feeling alienated and alone.

We start to habitually have negative thoughts about either ourselves or other people, which then attracts even more negative experiences into our lives. And so we deepen the vicious circle of negativity, invariably totally unaware that we are reinforcing it ourselves, through our own negative thinking.

During school age our peers tease us and sometimes bully us about the way we look, so we lose the whole-body-consciousness that all babies are born with, starting to feel separate from and often critical of our body. It doesn't run fast enough, it can't catch every ball that's thrown at us, it looks wrong.

When we are hurt, afraid, upset or angry, we may not understand the emotion but we feel these overwhelming sensations in our body, and consequently start to fear, blame or dislike what our body is experiencing, continuing to spiral outwards and downwards, away from our true centre and our natural connection with our body.

For the same reason, as a child we are unable to handle our strong feelings unless we are treated in a very loving and respectful way by our parents, and so we also start to distance ourselves from our feelings, believing ourselves to be wrong or bad for feeling angry, jealous, critical, afraid, depressed or any other strong emotion.

This journey usually continues in the same outward and downward spiralling direction throughout our youth and young adulthood. Indeed for many people their lives continue in this direction away from their centre and inner knowing for the rest of their lives, remaining for ever alienated from their feelings and distanced from their True Self.

For those lucky enough to experience some kind of spiritual awakening, or those who start to study wholistic personal development, and decide they are ready to grow and change in order to reach their full potential, a moment of enlightened awakening happens. I was lucky enough to experience this in my thirties when I started to study Psychosynthesis and heard I actually had a Higher Self that loved me exactly as I am.

These types of experiences and learnings connect us to the True Light of the Sun that awakens in our Spirit (see Fig.4). We turn on the Inner Light Bulb! This inner awakening radically changes the direction of our lives and we start the long journey back home. In the same way as the hero in Paulo Coelho's "The Alchemist" discovered, on completion of his quest, his treasure lay right back in the exact spot where he had come from!

And so we start on our Hero's Journey of completing the Spiral of Wholeness, and reversing the direction of the Spiral.

However even after having had an awakening experience, our path home is not always straightforward. We can so easily become trapped by the illusion of superiority and separation, which an unbalanced spirituality can bring. We may become "so heavenly we are of no earthly use"!

We can easily become even further from our centre and wholeness if we allow our new found spiritual awareness to make us lose touch with our logical thinking processes, or lose connection to our body's health, material and financial needs, or negate our emotions by insisting we "need to rise above them". All these deviations on the path can keep us away from our journey back to our centre, to our wholeness, and we may be side-tracked by some of these false beliefs for many years, or even decades. I know, I was!

One of the main reasons we struggle to finally free ourselves from our past limitations is because we all have a sub-personality (in the words of Psychosynthesis[9]) or a Part (in the words of NLP[10]) that can be called "The Self Saboteur". So the last exercise in this book is an exercise adapted from NLP, and is entitled "Transforming and Healing the Self Saboteur".

If you are new to NLP this may seem a little complicated, so before you try to do the exercise I have given an abbreviated example from some inner work I did recently. A difficult situation had arisen between myself and a friend, and by way of helping me to resolve the issue in my own head, I did this exercise.

I have a Self-Saboteur whose main job seems to be pleasing others, often to the detriment of myself. I am now good at being assertive, enough to stop any truly abusive behaviour coming my way, but my issue is after standing up for myself I then often feel guilty for being so "horrible" to them, and proceed to beat myself up mentally. This leaves me open to letting them "guilt-trip" me, ending up with both of us believing it was my fault in the first place, which couldn't actually be further from the truth.

I found this exercise to be so helpful, I realised it hadn't only made me feel better, but was also the right exercise with which to finally complete the writing of this book! It is truly amazing when we are centred and grounded in being held in the arms of a loving universe, even a seemingly negative experience will work together for the good of the whole.

So we can see it is only as we truly embrace every aspect of our self, our Mind, Body, Feelings and Spirit that we can finally **become whole!**

So here is my example.

Me	**My Self Saboteur**
1 What is your name and what do you look like?	*People Pleaser, kind and helpful, pleasant looking*
2 When did you first appear in my life?	*In the playground, aged 7-10 yrs*
3 What is your "Definition of Self" from your perspective?	
I am………	*kind*
Life is…..	*often difficult for people*
Others are…	*in need of my help*
4 What is your purpose in my life?	*To enable you to be of service*

5 How have you served me?	*By bringing joy into your life through your career, and your love of helping others*
6 What is the learning you are bringing to me as you are now?	*To teach you the first person you have a duty to please and be of service to is yourself!*
7 What do you need from me, in order to feel so loved and accepted, that you are then able to transform into something truly helpful to me now?	*I need you to Please Yourself I need you to honour, respect accept your own needs, hopes and dreams, always able to speak your truth, despite the consequences.*
8 So now that I am able to give you what you need, what blessings will you bring into my life in the future?	*You will no longer be able to be "guilt-tripped", when others are behaving badly but seeking to put the blame on to you*
9 Transformed Self Definition	
I am…….	*Wise enough to honour my needs first and foremost, realising I can only be there for others when I am truly able to be there for myself*
Life is…..	*A wonderful chance for us all to learn the lessons we have come to learn, me included!*

Others are….	*Sometimes able to benefit from my help and sometimes not! It is always their choice.*

Before doing this final exercise I would like you to pause and see if the next few lines feel true for you too.

I have just had a beautiful realisation with which I would like to conclude this book. When I stay centred in all four holistic perspectives, that means being centred in mind, body, feelings and spirit, then I am also centred in my heart. And my HEART is always open to LOVE because IT IS LOVE!

So as we find our way back to our True Centre we discover the most wonderful thing about this total journey to wholeness is that:-

WE DISCOVER WE ARE BACK IN OUR HEART SPACE

WE ARE ONCE AGAIN RE-CONNECTED TO LOVE

WE NOW KNOW WE ARE HELD SECURELY IN THE ARMS OF A LOVING UNIVERSE THAT HAS OUR BEST INTERESTS AT HEART.

AND WE HAVE BECOME WHOLE

Exercise Nine

Transforming and Healing the Self Saboteur

Ask this part of yourself if it is willing to enter into a dialogue with you and then imagine your Self Saboteur sitting in a chair opposite you and conversing with you. Write down its answers.

You	***The Self Saboteur***

1 What is your name and what do you look like?

2 When did you first appear in my life?

3 What is your "Definition of Self"

I am………

Life is…..

Others are…

4 What is your purpose in my life?

5 How have you served me in the past?

6 What is the learning you are bringing to me as you are now?

7 What do you need from me, in order to feel so loved and accepted, that you are then able to transform into something truly helpful to me now?

8 So now that I am able to give you what you need, what blessing will you bring into my life in the future?

9 Transformed Self Definition

I am…….

Life is…..

Others are….

Meditation Nine

Completing the Spiral of Wholeness Meditation

This is a visualisation meditation, so read it through first, noting all five stages of the journey in your journal as separate items, leaving space to fill in your experience afterwards. Firstly spend a few moments contemplating Fig. 4. Then allow your body to relax deeply, stilling your mind, and releasing any pressing emotions.

1. Become aware of yourself as a soul just prior to incarnation. Picture the diagram and imagine yourself becoming a tiny pinprick of light in the centre of the yellow circle. Feel yourself to be weightless, timeless, floating effortlessly in a loving, harmonious plane of existence……

2. Experience the sense of perfection. You have everything you need for your forthcoming journey in to this lifetime. Bask in the stillness, peace and beauty of this space…….

3. Contemplate what you may need when you descend to the earth plane. Ask for what you will need, knowing that every true desire will be granted, at some point during the life ahead of you, even if not totally in the way you envision…..

4. Listen for any words of encouragement, support or council from your loving Guides and helpers. Become

aware of any advice they have for you for the years ahead........

5. Watch yourself arriving in your new little body, and as you get born, grow, change, and develop into the person you are today. Watch this with a sense of acceptance and wholeness.

Take stock of any new insights, or awareness that this visualisation can bring into your consciousness to help you to heal any issues in your past and also face whatever situations are currently in your life or are about to come into your life in the near future.

About the Author

Emma Mary Gathergood trained as an occupational therapist in London in the 1960s and worked in the field of mental health. Being in close contact with those suffering trauma, anxiety and depression led her to study more holistic approaches to health, including Psychosynthesis. Already a practitioner of yoga and meditation, she realized the importance of including spiritual awareness with psychological growth in order to achieve full mental health.

She had time out to raise her family, during which period her interests widened into studying ancient wisdom, philosophy, healing and personal development. She travelled widely, spending time in India, New Zealand and America. In the 70s Emma ran the first Women's Consciousness Raising Group in Malvern, and in the 80s she was a Past Life Therapist in Glastonbury.

Emma Mary set up and ran a Stress Management business in the 90s, and later studied Life Coaching. On returning to work in a NHS psychiatric clinic, she continued her training by qualifying as an NLP practitioner, and studying Solution Focused Brief Therapy and also Mindfulness. Throughout her career Emma Mary has sought to empower people through an easily assimilated re-identification process, enabling her clients to dis-identify with their disabilities or weaknesses and re-identify with the Essence of who they truly are.

Her first book "Holistic Therapy – Overcoming Depression and Anxiety Naturally" has helped hundreds of people with its easy to understand message. Since retiring she has worked closely with the Wrekin Trust, a spiritual educational charity, influencing and developing its work "Whole Person – Whole World" through giving talks and a series of workshops. This book and CD are the latest development in her work.

To contact Emma Mary email emmag@wrekintrust.org or go to www.holisticlifecoach.org.uk

References

Chapter

1 1 Sir George Trevelyan in "Exploration unto God"

2 1 Albert Einstein see www.thinkexist.com

3 1 Barbara Marx Hubbard see www.barbaramarxhubbard.com

4 4 Steve Sisgold see www.wholebodyintelligence.com

5 4 Eugene Gendlin see www.focusing,org

6 4 Eugene Gendlin in "Focusing"

7 5 Claire Zammit and Kathryn Woodward Thomas see www.femininepower.com

8 6 Mindfulness see www.bangor.ac.uk/mindfulness

9 9 Psychosynthesis see www.psychosynthesis.edu

10 9 NLP see Jack Stewart, NLP Master Trainer

www.healingthespirit.eu

Other Works by the Same Author

Holistic Therapy Overcoming Depression and Anxiety Naturally

As a self-help guide the writing style is easy to follow, the text is engaging, really encouraging the reader to try out the exercises. There is a gap in the market for books like this. **Dr. Ian Johnson, Consultant Psychiatrist**

This book provides useful advice, is clearly written and is a very helpful guide. **David Lorimer Programme Director Scientific and Medical Network**

What a very useful, easy to read and understand handbag-sized book. How very informative particularly when one tries to make sense of the difference between the various therapeutic approaches, depressive feelings, anxiety and how the body responds to stress. It is a very gentle read and serves as a reflective tool for self-enquiry and healing. I like its holism and it is the fact it is an aide memoir for me. **Shirley Peters, Transpersonal Psychotherapist**

I loved every moment I spent immersed in this book. It was like re-discovering myself, in a very soothing and delightful way. It's helped me get a holistic perspective on my life and is packed with excellent practical approaches to managing thoughts and feelings and getting centred. I highly recommend this book whether you are in the mood for resolving a crisis or simply for joyous self-discovery. It's beautifully and accessibly written, with a perfect and reassuring balance of warmth, research and realism. **Will Thomas, Professional Coach, Bestselling and Award-winning Author**

Thanks so much for your book, Emma. You have a wonderful facility for clarifying complex subjects. **William Bloom, Author, Spiritual Teacher and Founder of Spiritual Companions**